CONTENTS

INTRODUCTION

My entire life can be summed up in three words: Weight loss diets. I tried every diet known to men – from keto and paleo diet to the cabbage soup diet. Seriously, I did it all. But the results were, to put it mildly, devastating. I want to lose weight no matter what it took because I was desperate. Over the years, I have found a few strategies that seem to be effective. However, they were short-lived and I have experienced weight cycling, also known as "yo-yo dieting". However, I did not know anything about food and nutrition. I did not know anything about my body and weight loss process. I didn't know that restrictive diets lead to increased appetite as the body loses muscle mass, trying to resupply depleted fat stores. Moreover, yo-yo dieting has harmful effects on our health; it has been associated with increased risk of heart diseases, diabetes, and fatty liver; in fact, weight fluctuations may be worse than staying overweight.

With this in mind, I decided to break the cycle of weight fluctuations with temporary success, and start thinking in terms of long-term lifestyle changes. First things first, I decide to change the way I cook my favorite food. I like home-cooked meals but I don't want to be occupied in the kitchen for hours. On the other hand, I like popular fast-food items such as burgers, French fries, pizza, and donuts. I wanted to drop my pounds but not miss out on my guilty pleasure foods. Therefore, an Air Fryer seemed to be working. I must confess, I was skeptical at first, but this small countertop convection oven seemed like a perfect solution to my problems with obesity and a great way to avoid consuming excessive calories. Besides being economical and practical, I found an Air Fryer perfect tool for family gatherings and children's birthday parties. Today, I can't imagine healthy dieting without an Air Fryer. It delivers a crispy finished product and flavor-packed meals without all that unhealthy oil. Isn't it fantastic?

In this cookbook, I have a tendency to promote a healthy lifestyle and traditional values, without starving and nutrient depletion. Family dinners bring families together, contributing to our physical and mental health. Did you know that a child who is engaged in the cooking process with parents is more likely to grow to be an adult who has healthy eating habits? This is the recipe collection I wish I had when I started my weight loss journey. It is all about my favorite Air Fryer recipes, including my personal experience with this unique kitchen tool. I started by making fried vegetables and chicken wings in it. Then I ventured into more complicated meals such as casserole and pastry. For this recipe collection, I chose easy-to-follow recipes with fewer ingredients so a family dinner can be a reality any night of the week. Are you searching for a way to simplify your cooking routine? Do you want recipes for the best "make-it-again" fried food? Well, you are in the right place. The Air Fryer and this recipe collection are ready to be your reliable kitchen companions! The Air Fryer will spark your imagination and create heart-warming family kitchen memories! Enjoy!

Getting to Know Your Air Fryer and Must-Know Tips

I'm asked two questions time and time again, "Why use an Air Fryer? Is an Air Fryer worth buying?" Well, I have three words for you: Health, convenience, and versatility. Everyone likes the taste of fried foods. Nothing says Saturday movie night better than a big bowl of chips! An air fryer is a modern kitchen appliance, a type of a mini convection oven, used for making fried foods. It offers a flavorful, crispy finished product by circulating hot air in the cooking chamber. In other words, a super-heated air circulates around your food for faster and even cooking results. An Air Fryer promises to take a place of a convection oven, deep fryer, grill, and microwave; this magical appliance also lets you sauté and roast your foods. The best of all – your food does not taste like fat. The Air Fryer uses rapid air technology to cook foods to perfection (crispy exteriors and well-cooked, moist interiors) with a drizzle of healthy oil.

Here are a few tips and hacks you might benefit from:

Needless to say, read the user's manual to make the most of your Air Fryer, even if you are an experienced cook; moreover, it is recommended to consult the manual every now and then, since there are dozens of different models of Air Fryer on the market.

If you are not in a hurry, preheat your Air Fryer to ensure even cooking. Turn it to the desired temperature and allow it to run for around 3 minutes before adding ingredients to the cooking basket.

Do not forget to grease the cooking basket; just brush the cooking basket lightly with a healthy oil; most Air Fryer recipes call for 1/2 teaspoon or less per serving.

Don't overcrowd the basket to promote even cooking; simply cook in batches and shake the basket periodically; you can spritz your food with a nonstick spray halfway through cooking time. One more thing – avoid cooking light items in the Air Fryer since it has a powerful fan on top of the unit, aggressively pushing hot air around your food, through the whole cooking basket. It includes leafy things like spinach and fresh herbs, seasonings, top slices of bread on sandwiches.

You can use your Air Fryer for healthy baked goods such as breakfast pastries and desserts. A 6-in round baking pan and bundt pan are worth investing in; bear in mind that baking pans should fit right inside the cooking basket.

Top Benefits of an Air Fryer You Need to Know

Fast and easy meals.

My Air Fryer helps me to avoid "there's-nothing-to-eat" situation on weeknights. Besides being a next-generation kitchen device, the Air Fryer frees up my time. It has automatic functions, so you don't need to stir food and watch the whole cooking process. Most of the recipes call for shaking the basket or flipping the ingredients halfway through the cooking time. That's it! When the cooking process ends, your Air Fryer will automatically turn off. The Air Fryer can deliver amazing results with minimal hands-on time.

Healthy fast food (improve your health and lose weight).

Really?! Is there such a thing as a healthy fast food? The truth is that it's practically impossible to follow a well-balanced diet when you're eating regularly junk food. On the other hand, cooking at home is associated with healthy eating habits. Your dietary patterns are extremely important on your weight loss journey. The good news is that you can cook French fries, donuts, fish, and burgers in your Air Fryer. This is only the beginning. Hearty casseroles, delicious appetizers, and delectable desserts will turn out great in your Air Fryer. When it comes to healthy weight loss that does not compromise flavor, this revolutionary kitchen gadget is a real winner! A lower intake of unhealthy oil is one of the greatest benefits of the Air Fryer. Fried food tastes good, right?! But trans fats are harmful to our health. Fried foods such as chicken nuggets, refrigerated dough, and rolls are high in trans fats. There are numerous negative health effects of eating deep-fried foods such as cardiovascular and coronary diseases, diabetes, obesity, gut microbes, and so on. According to the leading experts, when it comes to healthy dieting, you should not be afraid of fats. You should avoid partially hydrogenated and genetically modified oils such as cottonseed oil, corn oil, and margarine. Good fats include olive oil, avocado oil, nuts and seeds.

There are numerous benefits of cooking at home. You can control your portion and count calories more precisely; you can cook with natural and local ingredients. As you probably already know, most pre-packaged foods are high in salt, sodium, sugar and artificial ingredients. Did you know that the spills of used oils injure wildlife, which has harmful effects on our environment? Therefore, our food choices have a direct impact on our health and well-being.

A practical solution to every cooking challenge.

One of the greatest things I love about my Air Fryer is the fact that it cooks food in the sealed environment; it means you can forget about unpleasant kitchen smells! The Air Fryer is good at performing multiple tasks in the kitchen – frying, roasting, grilling, and baking. Some extra-large models can be used for a rotisserie and dehydrating. Plus, unlike the heat in your oven, the heat in the Air Fryer cooking basket is constant; it promotes better and even cooking.

It saves you time and money.

In today's fast-paced world, it seems difficult to follow a healthy diet. I know it. The Air Fryer is a massive time saver. Its easy press-and-go functions save a lot of time in the kitchen. If you're a practical person who doesn't want to spend a fortune on takeaways, you should invest in an Air Fryer. There are many money-saving kitchen tips out there; opt for freezer-friendly recipes that call for local and seasonal ingredients. You can look for items on sale or buy them in bulk. If you have leftover grains or beans, you can make delicious vegan burgers and freeze them in storage containers. This is far less expensive than eating out. The Air Fryer is an energy-efficient kitchen appliance too. To sum up, this is a space, cost, and frustration-saving cooking solution!

Do not give up eating fried foods, your Air Fryer is the perfect alternative to your favorite take-outs and restaurant. If you are thinking of cutting down on fat consumption, the Air Fryer is your number one choice! This is arguably the best way to cook fast food at your own kitchen and eat healthier. I hope you won't run out of inspiration with these 600 recipes! Happy air frying!

VEGETABLES & SIDE DISHES

Tomato and Cheese Stuffed Peppers

(Ready in about 13 minutes | Servings 3)

Per serving: 223 Calories; 6.5g Fat; 31.5g Carbs; 6.6g Protein; 17.7g Sugars; 8.5g Fiber

Ingredients

3 bell peppers, seeded and halved
1 tablespoon olive oil
1 small onion, chopped
2 garlic cloves, minced
Sea salt and ground black pepper, to taste
1 cup tomato sauce
2 ounces cheddar cheese, shredded

Directions

Toss the peppers with the oil; place them in the Air Fryer cooking basket.

Mix the onion, garlic, salt, black pepper, and tomato sauce. Spoon the sauce into the pepper halves.

Cook the peppers at 400 degrees F for about 10 minutes. Top the peppers with the cheese. Continue to cook for 5 minutes more.

Bon appétit!

Easy Parsnip Burgers

(Ready in about 20 minutes | Servings 3)

Per serving: 179 Calories; 2.2g Fat; 35.9g Carbs; 4.9g Protein; 5.6g Sugars; 6.5g Fiber

Ingredients

3/4 pound peeled parsnips, shredded
1/4 cup all-purpose flour
1/4 cup cornflour
1 egg, lightly beaten
1 teaspoon cayenne pepper
Sea salt and ground black pepper, to taste

Directions

Mix all ingredients until everything is well combined. Form the mixture into three patties.

Cook the burgers at 380 degrees F for about 15 minutes or until cooked through.

Bon appétit!

Classic Broccoli Salad

(Ready in about 8 minutes | Servings 3)

Per serving: 293 Calories; 24.3g Fat; 16.2g Carbs; 6.2g Protein; 6g Sugars; 4.6g Fiber

Ingredients

3/4 pound broccoli florets
1/4 cup raw sunflower seeds
1 clove garlic, peeled and minced
1 small red onion, thinly sliced
1/4 cup dried cranberries
1/4 cup extra-virgin olive oil
2 tablespoons fresh lemon juice
1 tablespoon Dijon mustard
Sea salt and ground black pepper, to taste

Directions

Place the broccoli florets in a lightly greased Air Fryer basket.

Cook the broccoli florets at 395 degrees F for 6 minutes, shaking the basket halfway through the cooking time.

Toss the broccoli florets with the remaining ingredients. Serve at room temperature.

Bon appétit!

Parmesan Cauliflower Florets

(Ready in about 15 minutes | Servings 4)

Per serving: 213 Calories; 15.3g Fat; 10.9g Carbs; 10.5g Protein; 2.6g Sugars; 2.8g Fiber

Ingredients

1 pound cauliflower florets
2 tablespoons olive oil
1 teaspoon smoked paprika
Sea salt and ground black pepper, to taste
4 ounces parmesan cheese, grated

Directions

Toss the cauliflower florets with the olive oil and spices. Toss until they are well coated on all sides.

Arrange the cauliflower florets in the Air Fryer basket.

Cook the cauliflower florets at 400 degrees F for about 13 minutes, shaking the basket halfway through the cooking time.

Toss the warm cauliflower florets with cheese. Bon appétit!

Parmesan Paprika Potatoes

(Ready in about 20 minutes | Servings 3)

Per serving: 215 Calories; 10g Fat; 24.3g Carbs; 8g Protein; 1.8g Sugars; 3g Fiber

Ingredients

3/4 pound potatoes, diced

1 tablespoon olive oil

1 teaspoon smoked paprika

1 teaspoon red pepper flakes, crushed

Sea salt and ground black pepper, to taste

2 ounces parmesan cheese, grated

Directions

Toss the potatoes with the olive oil and spices until well coated on all sides.

Arrange the potatoes in the Air Fryer basket.

Cook the potatoes at 400 degrees F for about 15 minutes, shaking the basket halfway through the cooking time.

Top the warm potatoes with cheese and serve immediately. Enjoy!

Szechuan Green Beans

(Ready in about 9 minutes | Servings 4)

Per serving: 108 Calories; 6.8g Fat; 10.7g Carbs; 3.4g Protein; 5g Sugars; 3.8g Fiber

Ingredients

1 pound fresh green beans, trimmed

1 tablespoon sesame oil

1/2 teaspoon garlic powder

1 tablespoon soy sauce

Sea salt and Szechuan pepper, to taste

2 tablespoons sesame seeds, lightly toasted

Directions

Toss the green beans with the sesame oil and garlic powder; then, arrange them in the Air Fryer basket.

Cook the green beans at 380 degrees F for 7 minutes; make sure to check the green beans halfway through the cooking time.

Toss the green beans with the remaining ingredients and stir to combine well. Enjoy!

Carrots with Sesame Seeds

(Ready in about 20 minutes | Servings 3)

Per serving: 131 Calories; 9.5g Fat; 11.1g Carbs; 1.7g Protein; 5.3g Sugars; 3.5g Fiber

Ingredients

3/4 pound carrots, trimmed and cut into sticks
2 tablespoons butter, melted
Coarse sea salt and white pepper, to taste
1 tablespoon sesame seeds, lightly toasted

Directions

Toss the carrots with the butter, salt, and white pepper; then, arrange them in the Air Fryer basket.

Cook the carrots at 380 degrees F for 15 minutes; make sure to check the carrots halfway through the cooking time.

Top the carrots with the sesame seeds. Bon appétit!

Warm Brussels Sprout Salad

(Ready in about 12 minutes | Servings 3)

Per serving: 138 Calories; 9.3g Fat; 12g Carbs; 4g Protein; 3.4g Sugars; 4.6g Fiber

Ingredients

3/4 pound Brussels sprouts, trimmed
2 tablespoons olive oil
Sea salt and ground black pepper, to taste
1/2 teaspoon dried dill weed
1 tablespoon fresh lemon juice
1 tablespoon rice vinegar

Directions

Toss the Brussels sprouts with the olive oil and spices until they are well coated on all sides; then, arrange the Brussels sprouts in the Air Fryer basket.

Cook the Brussels sprouts at 380 degrees F for 10 minutes, shaking the basket halfway through the cooking time.

Toss the Brussels sprouts with lemon juice and vinegar. Enjoy!

Dilled Buttery Sweet Potatoes

(Ready in about 40 minutes | Servings 2)

Per serving: 163 Calories; 5.8g Fat; 26.2g Carbs; 2g Protein; 5.4g Sugars; 3.6g Fiber

Ingredients

2 sweet potatoes, peeled and halved

1 tablespoon butter, melted

1 teaspoon dried dill weed

Sea salt and red pepper flakes, crushed

Directions

Toss the sweet potatoes with the remaining ingredients.

Cook the sweet potatoes at 380 degrees F for 15 minutes, shaking the basket halfway through the cooking time.

Taste and adjust the seasonings. Bon appétit!

Easy Buttery Mushrooms with Tomatoes

(Ready in about 10 minutes | Servings 4)

Per serving: 84 Calories; 6.3g Fat; 6.1g Carbs; 2.8g Protein; 2g Sugars; 4.1g Fiber

Ingredients

1 pound cremini mushrooms, sliced

1 large tomato, sliced

2 tablespoons butter, melted

1 teaspoon rosemary, minced

1 teaspoon parsley, minced

1 teaspoon garlic, minced

Coarse sea salt and ground black pepper, to taste

Directions

Toss the mushrooms and tomatoes with the remaining ingredients. Toss until they are well coated on all sides.

Arrange the mushrooms in the Air Fryer basket.

Cook your mushrooms at 400 degrees F for about 7 minutes, shaking the basket halfway through the cooking time.

Bon appétit!

Winter Vegetable Patties

(Ready in about 20 minutes | Servings 3)

Per serving: 184 Calories; 3.3g Fat; 31.1g Carbs; 8g Protein; 5.6g Sugars; 4.3g Fiber

Ingredients

1 carrot, shredded
1 parsnip, shredded
1 onion, chopped
1 garlic clove, minced
1/2 cup all-purpose flour
1 teaspoon cayenne pepper
Sea salt and ground black pepper, to taste
2 eggs, whisked

Directions

Mix all ingredients until everything is well combined. Form the mixture into three patties.

Cook the burgers at 380 degrees F for about 15 minutes or until cooked through.

Bon appétit!

Asian-Style Balsamic Fennel

(Ready in about 20 minutes | Servings 4)

Per serving: 114 Calories; 8.3g Fat; 9.1g Carbs; 2g Protein; 5.2g Sugars; 3.8g Fiber

Ingredients

1 pound fennel bulbs, trimmed and sliced
2 tablespoons sesame oil
Sea salt and ground black pepper, to taste
1 teaspoon red pepper flakes, crushed
1 tablespoon balsamic vinegar
1 tablespoon soy sauce
1 tablespoon sesame seeds, lightly toasted

Directions

Toss the fennel with the sesame oil, salt, black pepper, and red pepper flakes.

Cook the fennel at 370 degrees F for about 15 minutes or until cooked through; check your fennel halfway through the cooking time.

Toss the warm fennel with the vinegar, soy sauce, and sesame seeds.

Bon appétit!

Roasted Paprika Asparagus

(Ready in about 10 minutes | Servings 3)

Per serving: 110 Calories; 6.3g Fat; 9.2g Carbs; 2.9g Protein; 2.9g Sugars; 2.9g Fiber

Ingredients

3/4 pound fresh asparagus, trimmed

Coarse sea salt and ground black pepper, to taste

1 teaspoon paprika

2 tablespoons olive oil

Directions

Toss the asparagus with the salt, black pepper, paprika, and olive oil. Arrange the asparagus spears in the Air Fryer cooking basket.

Cook the asparagus at 400 degrees F for about 6 minutes, tossing them halfway through the cooking time.

Bon appétit!

Bean Buckwheat Burgers

(Ready in about 20 minutes | Servings 4)

Per serving: 198 Calories; 8.7g Fat; 24.2g Carbs; 8g Protein; 2.2g Sugars; 5.3g Fiber

Ingredients

1 cup buckwheat, soaked overnight and rinsed

1 cup canned kidney beans, drained and well rinsed

1/4 cup walnuts, chopped

1 tablespoon olive oil

1 small onion, chopped

1 teaspoon smoked paprika

Sea salt and ground black pepper, to taste

1/2 cup bread crumbs

Directions

Mix all ingredients until everything is well combined. Form the mixture into four patties and arrange them in a lightly greased Air Fryer basket.

Cook the burgers at 380 degrees F for about 15 minutes or until cooked through. Tun them over halfway through the cooking time.

Bon appétit!

Asparagus with Pecorino Cheese

(Ready in about 10 minutes | Servings 4)

Per serving: 120 Calories; 8.5g Fat; 5.9g Carbs; 6.9g Protein; 2.6g Sugars; 2.8g Fiber

Ingredients

1 pound asparagus, trimmed
1 tablespoon sesame oil
1/2 teaspoon onion powder
1/2 teaspoon granulated garlic
Sea salt and cayenne pepper, to taste
1/2 cup Pecorino cheese, preferably freshly grated

Directions

Toss the asparagus with the sesame oil, onion powder, granulated garlic, salt, and cayenne pepper. Arrange the asparagus spears in the Air Fryer cooking basket.

Cook the asparagus at 400 degrees F for about 6 minutes, tossing them halfway through the cooking time.

Top the asparagus with the cheese. Bon appétit!

Cheesy Green Beans

(Ready in about 9 minutes | Servings 2)

Per serving: 154 Calories; 9.6g Fat; 13g Carbs; 6.4g Protein; 6.9g Sugars; 3.4g Fiber

Ingredients

1/2 pound green beans
1 tablespoon sesame oil
Sea salt and ground black pepper, to taste
2 ounces cheddar cheese, grated

Directions

Toss the green beans with the sesame oil; then, arrange them in the Air Fryer basket.

Cook the green beans at 380 degrees F for 7 minutes, tossing the basket halfway through the cooking time.

Toss the warm green beans with the salt, black pepper, and cheese; stir to combine well. Enjoy!

Italian Peppers with Herbs

(Ready in about 15 minutes | Servings 3)

Per serving: 77 Calories; 4.6g Fat; 7.2g Carbs; 1.4g Protein; 5g Sugars; 2.4g Fiber

Ingredients

3 Italian peppers, seeded and halved
1 tablespoon olive oil
Kosher salt and ground black pepper, to taste
1 teaspoon cayenne pepper
1 tablespoon fresh parsley, chopped
1 tablespoon fresh basil, chopped
1 tablespoon fresh chives, chopped

Directions

Toss the peppers with the olive oil, salt, black pepper, and cayenne pepper; place the peppers in the Air Fryer cooking basket.

Cook the peppers at 400 degrees F for about 13 minutes, shaking the basket halfway through the cooking time.

Taste, adjust the seasonings, and serve with the fresh herbs. Bon appétit!

Brussels Sprouts with Ham

(Ready in about 15 minutes | Servings 4)

Per serving: 93 Calories; 4.3g Fat; 10.2g Carbs; 6.2g Protein; 2.4g Sugars; 4.3g Fiber

Ingredients

1 pound Brussels sprouts, trimmed
1 tablespoon peanut oil
Sea salt and freshly ground black pepper, to season
2 ounces ham, diced

Directions

Toss the Brussels sprouts with the remaining ingredients; then, arrange the Brussels sprouts in the Air Fryer basket.

Cook the Brussels sprouts at 380 degrees F for 13 minutes, shaking the basket halfway through the cooking time.

Serve warm and enjoy!

Buttery Garlicky Potatoes

(Ready in about 20 minutes | Servings 3)

Per serving: 123 Calories; 4g Fat; 20.1g Carbs; 2.3g Protein; 0.9g Sugars; 2.5g Fiber

Ingredients

3/4 pound potatoes, quartered
1 tablespoon butter, melted
1 teaspoon garlic, pressed
1 teaspoon dried oregano
Sea salt and ground black pepper, to taste

Directions

Toss the potatoes with the remaining ingredients until well coated on all sides.
Arrange the potatoes in the Air Fryer basket.
Cook the potatoes at 400 degrees F for about 18 minutes, shaking the basket halfway through the cooking time.
Serve warm and enjoy!

Cheesy Chestnut Mushrooms

(Ready in about 10 minutes | Servings 4)

Per serving: 83 Calories; 5.1g Fat; 6.4g Carbs; 4g Protein; 3.4g Sugars; 1.7g Fiber

Ingredients

1 pound chestnut mushrooms, quartered
1 tablespoon olive oil
1 garlic clove, pressed
Sea salt and ground black pepper, to taste
4 tablespoons Pecorino Romano cheese, shredded

Directions

Toss the mushrooms with the oil, garlic, salt, and black pepper. Toss until they are well coated on all sides.
Arrange the mushrooms in the Air Fryer basket.
Cook your mushrooms at 400 degrees F for about 7 minutes, shaking the basket halfway through the cooking time.
Afterwards, toss the mushrooms with the cheese and serve immediately!

Mexican-Style Sweet Potatoes

(Ready in about 40 minutes | Servings 4)

Per serving: 128 Calories; 3.5g Fat; 22.1g Carbs; 3g Protein; 2.1g Sugars; 3g Fiber

Ingredients

1 pound sweet potatoes, scrubbed, prick with a fork

1 tablespoon olive oil

Coarse sea salt and ground black pepper, to taste

1/2 teaspoon cayenne pepper

4 tablespoons salsa

Directions

Sprinkle the sweet potatoes with olive oil, salt, black pepper, and cayenne pepper.

Cook the sweet potatoes at 380 degrees F for 35 minutes, checking them halfway through the cooking time.

Split the tops open with a knife. Top each potato with salsa and serve. Bon appétit!

Brown Mushroom Burgers

(Ready in about 15 minutes | Servings 3)

Per serving: 184 Calories; 11.1g Fat; 14g Carbs; 9.4g Protein; 4g Sugars; 1.5g Fiber

Ingredients

3/4 pound brown mushrooms, chopped

1 large eggs, whisked

1/2 cup breadcrumbs

1/2 cup parmesan cheese, grated

1 small onion, minced

1 garlic clove, minced

Sea salt and ground black pepper, to taste

1 tablespoon olive oil

Directions

Mix all ingredients until everything is well combined. Form the mixture into three patties.

Cook the burgers at 380 degrees F for about 15 minutes or until cooked through.

Bon appétit!

Roasted Fennel Slices

(Ready in about 20 minutes | Servings 4)

Per serving: 97 Calories; 6.9g Fat; 8.4g Carbs; 1.4g Protein; 4.4g Sugars; 3.5g Fiber

Ingredients

1 pound fennel bulbs, trimmed and sliced
2 tablespoons olive oil
1 teaspoon fresh garlic, minced
1 teaspoon dried parsley flakes
Kosher salt and ground black pepper, to taste

Directions

Toss all ingredients in a mixing bowl.

Cook the fennel at 370 degrees F for about 15 minutes or until cooked through; check your fennel halfway through the cooking time.

Bon appétit!

Chinese Spicy Asparagus

(Ready in about 10 minutes | Servings 4)

Per serving: 75 Calories; 6g Fat; 5.6g Carbs; 2.8g Protein; 2.9g Sugars; 2.5g Fiber

Ingredients

1 pound asparagus
4 teaspoons Chinese chili oil
1/2 teaspoon garlic powder
1 tablespoon soy sauce
1/2 teaspoon red pepper flakes, crushed

Directions

Toss the asparagus with the remaining ingredients. Arrange the asparagus spears in the Air Fryer cooking basket.

Cook the asparagus at 400 degrees F for about 6 minutes, tossing them halfway through the cooking time.

Bon appétit!

Stuffed Breakfast Peppers

(Ready in about 15 minutes | Servings 3)

Per serving: 143 Calories; 9.1g Fat; 7.8g Carbs; 6.4g Protein; 5.4g Sugars; 2.6g Fiber

Ingredients

3 bell peppers, seeded and halved
1 tablespoon olive oil
3 eggs
3 tablespoons green onion, chopped
Sea salt and ground black pepper

Directions

Toss the peppers with the oil; place them in the Air Fryer cooking basket.
Crack an egg into each bell pepper half. Sprinkle your peppers with the salt and black pepper.
Cook the peppers at 400 degrees F for about 10 minutes. Top the peppers with green onions.
Continue to cook for 4 minutes more.
Bon appétit!

Indian Gujarati Green Beans

(Ready in about 10 minutes | Servings 3)

Per serving: 136 Calories; 10.4g Fat; 9.8g Carbs; 2.7g Protein; 4.9g Sugars; 3.3g Fiber

Ingredients

3/4 pound fresh green beans, trimmed
1 garlic clove, minced
2 tablespoons olive oil
1 tablespoon soy sauce
1 teaspoon black mustard seeds
1 dried red chile pepper, crushed
Sea salt and ground black pepper, to taste

Directions

Toss the green beans with the remaining ingredients; then, arrange them in the Air Fryer basket.
Cook the green beans at 380 degrees F for 8 minutes, tossing the basket halfway through the cooking time.
Enjoy!

Cheese Stuffed Mushrooms

(Ready in about 9 minutes | Servings 3)

Per serving: 124 Calories; 7.6g Fat; 8g Carbs; 7.7g Protein; 5g Sugars; 1.4g Fiber

Ingredients

3/4 pound button mushrooms, halved
1 tablespoon oil
Sea salt and ground black pepper, to taste
1/2 teaspoon garlic powder
3 ounces cheddar cheese, cubed

Directions

Toss the mushrooms with the olive oil, salt, black pepper, and garlic powder. Toss until they are well coated on all sides.
Arrange the mushrooms in the Air Fryer basket.
Cook your mushrooms at 400 degrees F for about 7 minutes, shaking the basket halfway through the cooking time.
Bon appétit!

Brussels Sprouts with Provolone Cheese

(Ready in about 13 minutes | Servings 4)

Per serving: 183 Calories; 11.3g Fat; 11.8g Carbs; 11.4g Protein; 3.2g Sugars; 4.5g Fiber

Ingredients

1 pound Brussels sprouts, trimmed
1 tablespoon olive oil
Sea salt and ground black pepper, to taste
4 ounces Provolone cheese, crumbled

Directions

Toss the Brussels sprouts with the olive oil and spices until they are well coated on all sides; then, arrange the Brussels sprouts in the Air Fryer basket.
Cook the Brussels sprouts at 380 degrees F for 10 minutes, shaking the basket halfway through the cooking time.
Toss the Brussels sprouts with the cheese and serve warm. Enjoy!

POULTRY

Chinese-Style Chicken Drumsticks

(Ready in about 25 minutes | Servings 3)

Per serving: 314 Calories; 22g Fat; 3.5g Carbs; 24.2g Protein; 1.8g Sugars; 0.5g Fiber

Ingredients

3 chicken drumsticks

2 tablespoons sesame oil

Kosher salt and ground black pepper, to taste

1 tablespoon soy sauce

1 teaspoon Five-spice powder

Directions

Pat the chicken drumsticks dry with paper towels. Toss the chicken drumsticks with the remaining ingredients.

Cook the chicken drumsticks at 370 degrees F for 22 minutes, turning them over halfway through the cooking time.

Bon appétit!

Sriracha Herb Turkey

(Ready in about 1 hour 5 minutes | Servings 5)

Per serving: 367 Calories; 21.9g Fat; 0.1g Carbs; 40g Protein; 0.2g Sugars; 0.2g Fiber

Ingredients

2 pounds turkey breasts, rib bones trimmed

4 tablespoons butter, melted

1 teaspoon Sriracha sauce

1 tablespoon fresh cilantro, chopped

1 tablespoon fresh parsley, chopped

1 tablespoon fresh thyme, chopped

Kosher salt and freshly ground black pepper, to taste

Directions

Pat the turkey breasts dry with paper towels. Toss the turkey breasts with the remaining ingredients.

Cook the turkey breasts at 350 degrees F for 1 hour, turning them over every 20 minutes.

Bon appétit!

Ranch Chicken Drumsticks

(Ready in about 25 minutes | Servings 4)

Per serving: 309 Calories; 17.2g Fat; 13.4g Carbs; 22.8g Protein; 0.4g Sugars; 0.8g Fiber

Ingredients

1/2 cup all-purpose flour

1 tablespoon Ranch seasoning mix

1 pound chicken drumsticks

1 tablespoon hot sauce

Sea salt and ground black pepper, to taste

Directions

Pat the chicken drumsticks dry with paper towels. Toss the chicken drumsticks with the remaining ingredients.

Cook the chicken drumsticks at 370 degrees F for 20 minutes, turning them over halfway through the cooking time.

Bon appétit!

Holiday Duck Roast

(Ready in about 45 minutes | Servings 5)

Per serving: 356 Calories; 11.7g Fat; 23.5g Carbs; 38.8g Protein; 15g Sugars; 5.1g Fiber

Ingredients

2 pounds duck breasts

1 tablespoon butter, melted

2 tablespoons pomegranate molasses

2 tablespoons miso paste

1 teaspoon garlic, minced

1 teaspoon ginger, peeled and minced

1 teaspoon Five-spice powder

Directions

Pat the duck breasts dry with paper towels. Toss the duck breast with the remaining ingredients.

Cook the duck breasts at 330 degrees F for 15 minutes, turning them over halfway through the cooking time.

Turn the heat to 350 degrees F; continue to cook for about 15 minutes or until cooked through.

Let it rest for 10 minutes before carving and serving. Bon appétit!

Sicilian Chicken Fillets

(Ready in about 20 minutes | Servings 4)

Per serving: 434 Calories; 32.4g Fat; 1.8g Carbs; 31.8g Protein; 0.7g Sugars; 0.5g Fiber

Ingredients

1 ½ pounds chicken fillets
2 tablespoons olive oil
1 teaspoon smoked paprika
1 teaspoon Italian seasoning mix
Sea salt and ground black pepper, to taste
1/2 cup Pecorino Romano cheese, grated

Directions

Pat the chicken fillets dry with paper towels. Toss the chicken fillets with the olive oil and spices.
Cook the chicken fillets at 380 degrees F for 12 minutes, turning them over halfway through the cooking time.
Top the chicken fillets with grated cheese and serve warm. Bon appétit!

Restaurant-Style Chicken Nuggets

(Ready in about 15 minutes | Servings 4)

Per serving: 467 Calories; 19.4g Fat; 26.8g Carbs; 38.8g Protein; 4.3g Sugars; 4.9g Fiber

Ingredients

1 egg, whisked
1/4 cup all-purpose flour
1 cup seasoned breadcrumbs
1 tablespoon olive oil
Sea salt and ground black pepper, to taste
1 ½ pounds chicken breasts, cut into small pieces

Directions

Mix the egg and flour in a shallow bowl. In a separate bowl, whisk the breadcrumbs, olive oil, salt, and black pepper.
Dip the chicken breasts into the egg mixture. Then, roll the chicken breasts over the breadcrumb mixture.
Cook the chicken at 380 degrees F for 12 minutes, turning them over halfway through the cooking time.
Bon appétit!

The Best Turkey Taquitos Ever

(Ready in about 30 minutes | Servings 6)

Per serving: 249 Calories; 11.4g Fat; 13.3g Carbs; 22.8g Protein; 1.6g Sugars; 2g Fiber

Ingredients

1 pound turkey breasts, boneless and skinless
Kosher salt and freshly ground black pepper, to taste
1 clove garlic, minced
1 habanero pepper, minced
4 ounces Mexican cheese blend, shredded
6 small corn tortillas
1/2 cup salsa

Directions

Pat the turkey breasts dry with kitchen towels. Toss the turkey breasts with the salt and black pepper.

Cook the turkey breasts at 380 degrees F for 18 minutes, turning them over halfway through the cooking time.

Place the shredded chicken, garlic, habanero pepper, and cheese on one end of each tortilla. Roll them up tightly and transfer them to a lightly oiled Air Fryer basket.

Bake your taquitos at 360 degrees F for 6 minutes. Serve your taquitos with salsa and enjoy!

Mexican Taco Chicken Fingers

(Ready in about 20 minutes | Servings 4)

Per serving: 427 Calories; 23.1g Fat; 11.1g Carbs; 41.4g Protein; 0.6g Sugars; 0.9g Fiber

Ingredients

1 egg, whisked
1/2 cup parmesan cheese, preferably freshly grated
1/2 cup tortilla chips, crushed
1/2 teaspoon onion powder
1/2 teaspoon garlic powder
1 teaspoon red chili powder
1 ½ pounds chicken breasts, boneless skinless cut into strips

Directions

Whisk the egg in a shallow bowl. In a separate bowl, whisk the parmesan cheese, tortilla chips, onion powder, garlic powder, and red chili powder.

Dip the chicken pieces into the egg mixture. Then, roll the chicken pieces over the breadcrumb mixture.

Cook the chicken at 380 degrees F for 12 minutes, turning them over halfway through the cooking time.

Bon appétit!

Classic Turkey Schnitzel

(Ready in about 25 minutes | Servings 3)

Per serving: 579 Calories; 27.4g Fat; 30.3g Carbs; 51g Protein; 2g Sugars; 1.6g Fiber

Ingredients

1 ½ pounds turkey thighs, skinless, boneless
1 egg, beaten
1/2 cup all-purpose flour
1/2 cup seasoned breadcrumbs
1/2 teaspoon red pepper flakes, crushed
Sea salt and ground black pepper, to taste
1 tablespoon olive oil

Directions

Flatten the turkey thighs with a mallet.

Whisk the egg in a shallow bowl. Place the flour in a second bowl.

Then, in a third shallow bowl, place the breadcrumbs, red pepper, salt, and black pepper. Dip the turkey first in the flour, then, in the beaten egg, and roll them in the breadcrumb mixture.

Place the breaded turkey thighs in the Air Fryer basket. Mist your schnitzel with the olive oil and transfer them to the cooking basket.

Cook the schnitzel at 380 degrees F for 22 minutes, turning them over halfway through the cooking time.

Bon appétit!

The Best Marinated Chicken Ever

(Ready in about 15 minutes + marinating time | Servings 2)

Per serving: 313 Calories; 16g Fat; 3.7g Carbs; 36.5g Protein; 2g Sugars; 0.9g Fiber

Ingredients

3/4 pound chicken breasts, boneless, skinless
1 teaspoon garlic, minced
1/2 cup red wine
1/4 cup hot sauce
1 tablespoon Dijon mustard
Sea salt and cayenne pepper, to taste

Directions

Place the chicken, garlic, red wine, hot sauce, and mustard in a ceramic bowl. Cover the bowl and let the chicken marinate for about 3 hours in your refrigerator.

Discard the marinade and place the chicken breasts in the Air Fryer cooking basket.

Cook the chicken breasts at 380 degrees F for 12 minutes, turning them over halfway through the cooking time.

Season the chicken with the salt and cayenne pepper to taste. Bon appétit!

Crispy Chicken Wings

(Ready in about 15 minutes | Servings 2)

Per serving: 265 Calories; 11.7g Fat; 0.5g Carbs; 37.5g Protein; 0.5g Sugars; 0.9g Fiber

Ingredients

3/4 pound chicken wings, boneless
1 tablespoon butter, room temperature
1/2 teaspoon garlic powder
1/2 teaspoon shallot powder
1/2 teaspoon mustard powder

Directions

Toss the chicken wings with the remaining ingredients.

Cook the chicken wings at 380 degrees F for 18 minutes, turning them over halfway through the cooking time.

Bon appétit!

Country-Style Turkey Drumsticks

(Ready in about 45 minutes | Servings 5)

Per serving: 341 Calories; 21.7g Fat; 0.5g Carbs; 35.5g Protein; 0.1g Sugars; 0.1g Fiber

Ingredients

2 pounds turkey drumsticks, bone-in
2 tablespoons olive oil
Kosher salt and freshly ground black pepper, to taste
1 teaspoon dried thyme
1 teaspoon dried rosemary
1 teaspoon garlic, minced

Directions

Toss the turkey drumsticks with the remaining ingredients.

Cook the turkey drumsticks at 400 degrees F for 40 minutes, turning them over halfway through the cooking time.

Bon appétit!

Peppery Chicken Fillets

(Ready in about 20 minutes | Servings 4)

Per serving: 305 Calories; 22.8g Fat; 2.3g Carbs; 21.6g Protein; 1.1g Sugars; 0.4g Fiber

Ingredients

1 pound chicken fillets

2 tablespoons butter

2 bell peppers, seeded and sliced

1 teaspoon garlic, minced

Sea salt and ground black pepper, to taste

1 teaspoon red pepper flakes

Directions

Toss the chicken fillets with the butter and place them in the Air Fryer basket. Top the chicken with bell peppers, garlic, salt, black pepper, and red pepper flakes.

Cook the chicken and peppers at 380 degrees F for 15 minutes, tossing the basket halfway through the cooking time.

Serve warm and enjoy!

Traditional Orange Duck

(Ready in about 45 minutes | Servings 4)

Per serving: 471 Calories; 44.1g Fat; 2.9g Carbs; 13.3g Protein; 2.1g Sugars; 0.3g Fiber

Ingredients

1 pound duck legs

1/4 cup orange sauce

Sea salt and red pepper flakes, crushed

Directions

Toss the duck legs with the remaining ingredients.

Cook the duck legs at 400 degrees F for 40 minutes, turning them over halfway through the cooking time.

Bon appétit!

Chicken Dinner Rolls

(Ready in about 20 minutes | Servings 4)

Per serving: 575 Calories; 25.3g Fat; 37g Carbs; 49.7g Protein; 4.6g Sugars; 3.2g Fiber

Ingredients

1 pound chicken, ground
1/2 cup tortilla chips, crushed
2 ounces cheddar cheese, grated
1 teaspoon dried parsley flakes
1 teaspoon cayenne pepper
1/2 teaspoon paprika
Kosher salt and ground black pepper, to taste
4 dinner rolls

Directions

Mix the chicken, tortilla chips, cheese, and spices until everything is well combined. Now, roll the mixture into four patties.

Cook the burgers at 380 degrees F for about 17 minutes or until cooked through; make sure to turn them over halfway through the cooking time.

Serve your burgers in dinner rolls. Bon appétit!

Ham and Cheese Stuffed Chicken

(Ready in about 25 minutes | Servings 4)

Per serving: 486 Calories; 32.3g Fat; 7.9g Carbs; 39.3g Protein; 0.8g Sugars; 0.2g Fiber

Ingredients

1 pound chicken breasts, skinless, boneless and cut into 4 slices
4 ounces goat cheese, crumbled
4 ounces ham, chopped
1 egg
1/4 cup all-purpose flour
1/4 cup parmesan cheese, grated
1/2 teaspoon onion powder
1/2 teaspoon garlic powder

Directions

Flatten the chicken breasts with a mallet.

Stuff each piece of chicken with cheese and ham. Roll them up and secure with toothpicks.

In a shallow bowl, mix the remaining ingredients until well combined. Dip the chicken rolls into the egg/flour mixture.

Place the stuffed chicken in the Air Fryer cooking basket. Cook the stuffed chicken breasts at 400 degrees F for about 22 minutes, turning them over halfway through the cooking time.

Bon appétit!

Parsley Lemon Turkey

(Ready in about 45 minutes | Servings 5)

Per serving: 411 Calories; 27.8g Fat; 1.3g Carbs; 36.5g Protein; 0.3g Sugars; 0.2g Fiber

Ingredients

2 pounds turkey wings
2 tablespoons olive oil
1/2 teaspoon garlic powder
1/2 teaspoon onion powder
1 teaspoon poultry seasoning mix
2 tablespoons fresh parsley, roughly chopped
1 lemon, cut into slices

Directions

Toss the turkey wings with the olive oil, garlic powder, onion powder, and poultry seasoning mix.

Cook the turkey wings at 400 degrees F for 40 minutes, turning them over halfway through the cooking time.

Let the turkey rest for 10 minutes before carving and serving. Garnish the turkey wings with the parsley and lemon slices.

Bon appétit!

Chicken Cutlets with Broccoli

(Ready in about 15 minutes | Servings 4)

Per serving: 313 Calories; 20.8g Fat; 7.5g Carbs; 24.5g Protein; 1.9g Sugars; 2g Fiber

Ingredients

1 pound chicken cutlets
1 pound broccoli florets
1 tablespoon olive oil
Sea salt and ground black pepper, to taste

Directions

Pat the chicken dry with kitchen towels. Place the chicken cutlets in a lightly greased Air Fryer basket.

Cook the chicken cutlets at 380 degrees F for 6 minutes, turning them over halfway through the cooking time.

Turn the heat to 400 degrees F and add in the remaining ingredients. Continue to cook for 6 minutes more.

Bon appétit!

Creamed Chicken Salad

(Ready in about 20 minutes | Servings 4)

Per serving: 315 Calories; 23g Fat; 2.8g Carbs; 24.5g Protein; 0.9g Sugars; 0.4g Fiber

Ingredients

1 pound chicken breasts, skinless and boneless

1/4 cup mayonnaise

1/4 cup sour cream

1 tablespoon lemon juice

Sea salt and ground black pepper

1/2 cup celery, chopped

Directions

Pat the chicken dry with paper towels. Place the chicken in a lightly oiled cooking basket.

Cook the chicken breasts at 380 degrees F for 12 minutes, turning them over halfway through the cooking time.

Shred the chicken breasts using two forks; transfer it to a salad bowl and add in the remaining ingredients.

Toss to combine and serve well chilled. Bon appétit!

Tender Spicy Chicken

(Ready in about 15 minutes + marinating time | Servings 4)

Per serving: 206 Calories; 11g Fat; 1g Carbs; 24.2g Protein; 0.4g Sugars; 0.2g Fiber

Ingredients

1 pound chicken breasts, boneless, skinless

1/2 cup rice wine

1 tablespoon stone-ground mustard

1 teaspoon garlic, minced

1 teaspoon black peppercorns, whole

1 teaspoon chili powder

1/4 teaspoon sea salt, or more to taste

Directions

Place the chicken, wine, mustard, garlic, and whole peppercorns in a ceramic bowl. Cover the bowl and let the chicken marinate for about 3 hours in your refrigerator.

Discard the marinade and place the chicken breasts in the Air Fryer cooking basket.

Cook the chicken breasts at 380 degrees F for 12 minutes, turning them over halfway through the cooking time.

Season the chicken with the chili powder and salt. Serve immediately and enjoy!

Ranch Chicken Wings

(Ready in about 25 minutes | Servings 3)

Per serving: 273 Calories; 14.3g Fat; 0.5g Carbs; 33.2g Protein; 0.4g Sugars; 0.5g Fiber

Ingredients

1 pound chicken wings, boneless
2 tablespoons olive oil
1 teaspoon Ranch seasoning mix
Kosher salt and ground black pepper, to taste

Directions

Pat the chicken dry with kitchen towels. Toss the chicken with the remaining ingredients.

Cook the chicken wings at 380 degrees F for 22 minutes, turning them over halfway through the cooking time.

Bon appétit!

Roasted Turkey Legs with Scallions

(Ready in about 45 minutes | Servings 4)

Per serving: 279 Calories; 14.4g Fat; 1.8g Carbs; 33.6g Protein; 0.7g Sugars; 0.5g Fiber

Ingredients

1 ½ pounds turkey legs
1 tablespoon butter, melted
1 teaspoon hot paprika
1 teaspoon garlic, pressed
Sea salt and ground black pepper, to taste
2 tablespoons scallions, chopped

Directions

Toss the turkey legs with the remaining ingredients, except for the scallions.

Cook the turkey legs at 400 degrees F for 40 minutes, turning them over halfway through the cooking time.

Garnish the roasted turkey legs with the fresh scallions and enjoy!

Turkey and Avocado Sliders

(Ready in about 25 minutes | Servings 4)

Per serving: 519 Calories; 22.4g Fat; 48g Carbs; 31.6g Protein; 6.7g Sugars; 5g Fiber

Ingredients

1 pound turkey, ground
1 tablespoon olive oil
1 avocado, peeled, pitted and chopped
2 garlic cloves, minced
1/2 cup breadcrumbs
Kosher salt and ground black pepper, to taste
8 small rolls

Directions

Mix the turkey, olive oil, avocado, garlic, breadcrumbs, salt, and black pepper until everything is well combined. Form the mixture into eight small patties.

Cook the patties at 380 degrees F for about 20 minutes or until cooked through; make sure to turn them over halfway through the cooking time.

Serve your patties in the prepared rolls and enjoy!

Chicken Salad Sandwich

(Ready in about 20 minutes | Servings 4)

Per serving: 522 Calories; 31.4g Fat; 27.1g Carbs; 31.6g Protein; 5.2g Sugars; 2.5g Fiber

Ingredients

1 pound chicken breasts, boneless and skinless
1 stalks celery, chopped
1 carrot, chopped
1 small onion, chopped
1 cup mayonnaise
Sea salt and ground black pepper, to taste
4 sandwich buns

Directions

Pat the chicken dry with paper towels. Place the chicken in a lightly oiled cooking basket.

Cook the chicken breasts at 380 degrees F for 12 minutes, turning them over halfway through the cooking time.

Shred the chicken breasts using two forks; transfer it to a salad bowl and add in the celery, carrot, onion, mayo, salt, and pepper.

Toss to combine and serve in sandwich buns. Enjoy!

Italian-Style Chicken Drumsticks

(Ready in about 25 minutes | Servings 4)

Per serving: 235 Calories; 14.8g Fat; 0.3g Carbs; 23.2g Protein; 0.1g Sugars; 0.3g Fiber

Ingredients

4 chicken drumsticks, bone-in
1 tablespoon butter
1/2 teaspoon cayenne pepper
1 teaspoon Italian herb mix
Sea salt and ground black pepper, to taste

Directions

Pat the chicken drumsticks dry with paper towels. Toss the chicken drumsticks with the remaining ingredients.

Cook the chicken drumsticks at 370 degrees F for 20 minutes, turning them over halfway through the cooking time.

Bon appétit!

Thai Hot Chicken Drumettes

(Ready in about 25 minutes | Servings 3)

Per serving: 260 Calories; 13.3g Fat; 0.5g Carbs; 31.2g Protein; 0.4g Sugars; 0.5g Fiber

Ingredients

1 pound chicken drumettes, bone-in
Sea salt and freshly ground black pepper, to taste
1/4 cup Thai hot sauces
2 tablespoons sesame oil
1 teaspoon tamari sauce

Directions

Toss the chicken drumettes with the remaining ingredients.

Cook the chicken drumettes at 380 degrees F for 22 minutes, turning them over halfway through the cooking time.

Bon appétit!

Buttermilk Fried Chicken

(Ready in about 15 minutes + marinating time | Servings 4)

Per serving: 266 Calories; 3.9g Fat; 26.7g Carbs; 28.2g Protein; 3g Sugars; 0.8g Fiber

Ingredients

1 pound chicken breast halves
Sea salt and ground black pepper, to taste
1 cup buttermilk
1 cup all-purpose flour
1/2 teaspoon onion powder
1 teaspoon garlic powder
1 teaspoon smoked paprika

Directions

Toss together the chicken pieces, salt, and black pepper in a large bowl to coat. Stir in the buttermilk until the chicken is coated on all sides. Place the chicken in your refrigerator for about 6 hours.

In a shallow bowl, thoroughly combine the flour, onion powder, garlic powder, and smoked paprika.

Then, dredge the chicken in the seasoned flour; shake off any excess and transfer them to a lightly oiled Air Fryer basket.

Cook the chicken breasts at 380 degrees F for 12 minutes, turning them over halfway through the cooking time.

Enjoy!

BEEF

Classis Steak Salad

(Ready in about 15 minutes | Servings 5)

Per serving: 316 Calories; 16g Fat; 3.7g Carbs; 38.2g Protein; 1.7g Sugars; 0.7g Fiber

Ingredients

2 pounds T-bone steak
1 teaspoon garlic powder
Sea salt and ground black pepper, to taste
2 tablespoons lime juice
1/4 cup extra-virgin olive oil
1 bell pepper, seeded and sliced
1 red onion, sliced
1 tomato, diced

Directions

Toss the steak with the garlic powder, salt, and black pepper; place the steak in the Air Fryer cooking basket.

Cook the steak at 400 degrees F for 12 minutes, turning it over halfway through the cooking time.

Cut the steak into slices and add in the remaining ingredients. Serve at room temperature or well-chilled.

Bon appétit!

Easy Beef Sliders

(Ready in about 20 minutes | Servings 4)

Per serving: 406 Calories; 16.2g Fat; 27g Carbs; 35.2g Protein; 1.5g Sugars; 2.6g Fiber

Ingredients

1 pound ground beef
1/2 teaspoon garlic powder
1/2 teaspoon onion powder
1 teaspoon paprika
Sea salt and ground black pepper, to taste
8 dinner rolls

Directions

Mix all ingredients , except for the dinner rolls. Shape the mixture into four patties.

Cook the burgers at 380 degrees F for about 15 minutes or until cooked through; make sure to turn them over halfway through the cooking time.

Serve your burgers on the prepared dinner rolls and enjoy!

Tender Buttery Filet Mignon

(Ready in about 20 minutes | Servings 4)

Per serving: 393 Calories; 26.2g Fat; 2.7g Carbs; 36.2g Protein; 1.5g Sugars; 0.2g Fiber

Ingredients

1 ½ pounds filet mignon

2 tablespoons soy sauce

2 tablespoons butter, melted

1 teaspoon mustard powder

1 teaspoon garlic powder

Sea salt and ground black pepper, to taste

Directions

Toss the filet mignon with the remaining ingredients; place the filet mignon in the Air Fryer cooking basket.

Cook the filet mignon at 400 degrees F for 14 minutes, turning it over halfway through the cooking time.

Enjoy!

Christmas Corned Beef

(Ready in about 1 hour 10 minutes | Servings 4)

Per serving: 410 Calories; 32.4g Fat; 2.9g Carbs; 25.6g Protein; 0.8g Sugars; 0.9g Fiber

Ingredients

1 ½ pounds beef brisket

2 tablespoons olive oil

1 tablespoon smoked paprika

1 tablespoon English mustard powder

1 teaspoon ground

1 teaspoon chili pepper flakes

2 garlic cloves, pressed

Directions

Toss the beef with the remaining ingredients; place the beef in the Air Fryer cooking basket.

Cook the beef at 390 degrees F for 15 minutes, turn the beef over and reduce the temperature to 360 degrees F.

Continue to cook the beef for 55 minutes more. Bon appétit!

Beef Shoulder with Onion

(Ready in about 55 minutes | Servings 4)

Per serving: 309 Calories; 16.2g Fat; 2.2g Carbs; 36.2g Protein; 0.7g Sugars; 0.4g Fiber

Ingredients

1 ½ pounds beef shoulder
Sea salt and ground black pepper, to taste
1 teaspoon cayenne pepper
1/2 teaspoon ground cumin
2 tablespoons olive oil
2 cloves garlic, minced
1 teaspoon Dijon mustard
1 onion, cut into slices

Directions

Toss the beef with the spices, garlic, mustard, and olive oil; place the beef in a lightly oiled Air Fryer cooking basket.

Cook the beef at 390 degrees F for 45 minutes, turning it over halfway through the cooking time.

Add in the onion and continue to cook an additional 10 minutes.

Bon appétit!

Greek Pulled Beef (Gyros)

(Ready in about 1 hour 10 minutes | Servings 4)

Per serving: 402 Calories; 32.2g Fat; 1.2g Carbs; 25.2g Protein; 0.1g Sugars; 0.3g Fiber

Ingredients

1 ½ pounds beef brisket
2 tablespoons olive oil
Sea salt and freshly ground black pepper, to season
1 teaspoon dried oregano
1 teaspoon mustard powder
1/2 teaspoon ground cumin
2 cloves garlic, minced
2 tablespoons chives, chopped
2 tablespoons cilantro, chopped

Directions

Toss the beef brisket with the rest of the ingredients; now, place the beef brisket in the Air Fryer cooking basket.

Cook the beef brisket at 390 degrees F for 15 minutes, turn the beef over and reduce the temperature to 360 degrees F.

Continue to cook the beef brisket for approximately 55 minutes or until cooked through.

Shred the beef with two forks and serve with toppings of choice. Bon appétit!

Holiday Chuck Roast

(Ready in about 4 hours | Servings 5)

Per serving: 267 Calories; 11.5g Fat; 3g Carbs; 38.1g Protein; 0.8g Sugars; 0.4g Fiber

Ingredients

1/2 cup red wine

1 tablespoon Dijon mustard

1 tablespoon fresh garlic, minced

1 teaspoon red pepper flakes, crushed

Sea salt and ground black pepper, to taste

2 pounds chuck roast

1 tablespoon corn flour

Directions

Place the wine, mustard, garlic, red pepper, salt, black pepper, and chuck roast in a ceramic bowl. Cover the bowl and let the meat marinate for 3 hours in your refrigerator.

Toss the roast beef with the corn flour; place the roast beef in the Air Fryer cooking basket.

Cook the roast beef at 390 degrees F for 55 minutes, turning them over halfway through the cooking time.

Enjoy!

Chuck Eye Roast with Tomatoes

(Ready in about 55 minutes | Servings 4)

Per serving: 299 Calories; 17g Fat; 1.4g Carbs; 36.1g Protein; 0.8g Sugars; 0.4g Fiber

Ingredients

1 ½ pounds chuck eye roast

Sea salt and ground black pepper, to taste

1 teaspoon red pepper flakes, crushed

2 tablespoons olive oil, melted

1 jalapeno pepper, chopped

1 large-sized tomato, sliced

Directions

Toss the roast beef with the salt, black pepper, salt, red pepper flakes, and olive oil; place the roast beef in a lightly oiled Air Fryer cooking basket.

Cook the roast beef at 390 degrees F for 45 minutes, turning it over halfway through the cooking time.

Top the roast beef with the tomato and jalapeno pepper. Continue to cook for 10 minutes more.

Enjoy!

Smoked Beef Sausage with Peppers

(Ready in about 20 minutes | Servings 4)

Per serving: 464 Calories; 42g Fat; 3.5g Carbs; 16.1g Protein; 1g Sugars; 0.5g Fiber

Ingredients

1 pound smoked beef sausage
2 bell peppers, sliced
2 garlic cloves, pressed
2 tablespoons olive oil
1 teaspoon sage
1 teaspoon thyme
Sea salt and red pepper, to season

Directions

Toss all ingredients in a lightly oiled Air Fryer cooking basket.

Cook the sausage and peppers at 380 degrees F for 15 minutes, tossing the basket halfway through the cooking time.

Serve warm and enjoy!

Home-Style Mini Meatloaves

(Ready in about 25 minutes | Servings 4)

Per serving: 279 Calories; 14.5g Fat; 11.4g Carbs; 25.3g Protein; 0.8g Sugars; 0.6g Fiber

Ingredients

1 pound ground chuck
1 tablespoon olive oil
1 small-sized onion, chopped
2 garlic cloves, minced
1/4 cup breadcrumbs
1 egg, beaten
Sea salt and ground black pepper, to taste
1/2 cup ketchup

Directions

Thoroughly combine all ingredients , except for the ketchup; mix until everything is well combined.

Scrape the beef mixture into a lightly oiled muffin tin and transfer it to the Air Fryer cooking basket.

Cook your meatloaves at 380 degrees F for 20 minutes. Then, spread the ketchup over the top of the meatloaves. Continue cooking for another 5 minutes.

Bon appétit!

Herb Butter Steak

(Ready in about 15 minutes | Servings 5)

Per serving: 316 Calories; 18.1g Fat; 0.7g Carbs; 37.2g Protein; 0.1g Sugars; 0.1g Fiber

Ingredients

2 pounds ribeye steaks, bone-in

Kosher salt and freshly ground black pepper, to taste

3 tablespoons butter

1 tablespoon fresh basil, minced

1 tablespoon fresh parsley, minced

2 tablespoons fresh scallions, minced

2 cloves garlic, minced

Kosher salt and freshly ground black pepper, to taste

Directions

Toss the steak with the salt and black pepper; place the steak in a lightly oiled Air Fryer cooking basket.

Cook the steak at 400 degrees F for 12 minutes, turning it over halfway through the cooking time.

In the meantime, mix the butter with the remaining ingredients and place it in the refrigerator until well-chilled.

Serve the warm steak with the chilled herb butter and enjoy!

Restaurant-Style Ribeye Steak

(Ready in about 20 minutes | Servings 4)

Per serving: 451 Calories; 34.1g Fat; 3.4g Carbs; 33.2g Protein; 0.1g Sugars; 0.1g Fiber

Ingredients

1 ½ pounds ribeye steak

Sea salt and freshly ground black pepper, to taste

1 tablespoon olive oil

2 garlic cloves, minced

1/2 stick butter, cold and cut into cubes

Directions

Toss the ribeye steak with the salt, black pepper, olive oil, and garlic; place the ribeye steak in the Air Fryer cooking basket.

Cook the ribeye steak at 400 degrees F for 15 minutes, turning it over halfway through the cooking time.

Top the ribeye steak with the butter and serve warm. Bon appétit!

Beef and Broccoli Patties

(Ready in about 20 minutes | Servings 4)

Per serving: 252 Calories; 14.7g Fat; 7g Carbs; 24.2g Protein; 2.4g Sugars; 2.1g Fiber

Ingredients

1 pound beef

1/2 pound broccoli, minced

1 small onion, chopped

2 garlic cloves, minced

Sea salt and ground black pepper, to taste

1 tablespoon tamari sauce

Directions

In a mixing bowl, thoroughly combine all ingredients . Shape the mixture into four patties.

Cook the burgers at 380 degrees F for about 15 minutes or until cooked through; make sure to turn them over halfway through the cooking time.

Serve the warm patties with the topping of choice. Bon appétit!

Glazed Corned Beef

(Ready in about 1 hour 10 minutes | Servings 4)

Per serving: 362 Calories; 25.6g Fat; 5.9g Carbs; 25.8g Protein; 2.7g Sugars; 1.2g Fiber

Ingredients

1 ½ pounds beef brisket

2 tablespoons tomato ketchup

1 tablespoon brown mustard

1 teaspoon chili powder

2 tablespoons salt

1 teaspoon garlic powder

1 teaspoon onion powder

1 tablespoon ground black pepper

1 tablespoon brown sugar

Directions

Toss the beef with the remaining ingredients; place the beef in the Air Fryer cooking basket.

Cook the beef at 390 degrees F for 15 minutes, turn the beef over and reduce the temperature to 360 degrees F.

Continue to cook the beef for 55 minutes more or until cooked through Bon appétit!

Garlicky Roast Beef

(Ready in about 4 hours | Servings 4)

Per serving: 301 Calories; 11.5g Fat; 3g Carbs; 38.1g Protein; 0.8g Sugars; 0.4g Fiber

Ingredients

1 ½ pounds eye round roast

4 cloves garlic, peeled and thinly sliced

2 tablespoons olive oil

Kosher salt and ground black pepper, to taste

Directions

Pierce the beef with a sharp knife and insert the garlic slices into the holes.

Toss the meat with the oil, salt, and black pepper and transfer it to the Air Fryer cooking basket.

Cook the roast beef at 390 degrees F for 55 minutes, turning it over halfway through the cooking time.

Enjoy!

Butter and Allspice Coulotte Roast

(Ready in about 55 minutes | Servings 5)

Per serving: 300 Calories; 15.5g Fat; 1.3g Carbs; 37.1g Protein; 0.4g Sugars; 0.2g Fiber

Ingredients

2 pounds Coulotte roast

2 tablespoons butter

Kosher salt and ground black pepper, to taste

1 teaspoon ground allspice

1 teaspoon garlic, minced

Directions

Toss the beef with the remaining ingredients; place the beef in the Air Fryer cooking basket.

Cook the beef at 390 degrees F for 55 minutes, turning it over halfway through the cooking time.

Enjoy!

Parmesan Filet Mignon

(Ready in about 15 minutes | Servings 4)

Per serving: 382 Calories; 26.5g Fat; 4.9g Carbs; 31.1g Protein; 0.6g Sugars; 0.2g Fiber

Ingredients

1 pound filet mignon
Sea salt and ground black pepper, to season
1 teaspoon red pepper flakes
1 teaspoon rosemary, finely chopped
2 tablespoons olive oil
1 cup parmesan cheese, preferably freshly grated

Directions

Toss the filet mignon with the salt, black pepper, red pepper, rosemary, and olive oil; place the filet mignon in the Air Fryer cooking basket.

Cook the filet mignon at 400 degrees F for 14 minutes, turning it over halfway through the cooking time.

Enjoy!

Italian Pulled Pork Ragu

(Ready in about 1 hour 10 minutes | Servings 5)

Per serving: 259 Calories; 10.9g Fat; 2.5g Carbs; 37g Protein; 0.6g Sugars; 0.4g Fiber

Ingredients

2 pounds beef shoulder
Kosher salt and ground black pepper, to taste
2 garlic cloves, minced
1 tablespoon Italian seasoning mix

Directions

Toss the beef shoulder with the remaining ingredients; now, place the beef shoulder in the Air Fryer cooking basket.

Cook the beef shoulder at 390 degrees F for 15 minutes, turn the beef shoulder over and reduce the temperature to 360 degrees F.

Continue to cook the beef shoulder for approximately 55 minutes or until cooked through.

Shred the beef shoulder with two forks and serve with toppings of choice. Bon appétit!

Beef Sausage with Baby Potatoes

(Ready in about 20 minutes | Servings 4)

Per serving: 625 Calories; 33g Fat; 62.1g Carbs; 20.7g Protein; 2.6g Sugars; 7.4g Fiber

Ingredients

8 baby potatoes, scrubbed and halved
4 smoked beef sausages
1 teaspoon Italian seasoning mix

Directions

Toss all ingredients in a lightly oiled Air Fryer cooking basket.
Cook the sausage and potatoes at 400 degrees F for 15 minutes, tossing the basket halfway through the cooking time.
Serve warm and enjoy!

Beef Mushroom Breakfast Muffins

(Ready in about 30 minutes | Servings 4)

Per serving: 305 Calories; 17.1g Fat; 12.5g Carbs; 25.6g Protein; 8.1g Sugars; 0.8g Fiber

Ingredients

1 pound ground beef
1 egg, beaten
1 teaspoon Dijon mustard
Sea salt and ground black pepper, to taste
1/2 onion, minced
1/2 cup mushrooms
1/4 cup seasoned bread crumbs
1 teaspoon Italian seasoning mix
1/2 cup ketchup

Directions

Thoroughly combine all ingredients , except for the ketchup; mix until everything is well combined.
Scrape the beef mixture into lightly oiled silicone cups and transfer them to the Air Fryer cooking basket.
Cook your muffins at 380 degrees F for 20 minutes.
Then, spread the ketchup on the top of each muffin and continue cooking for another 5 minutes.
Bon appétit!

Dijon Chuck Eye Steak

(Ready in about 15 minutes | Servings 4)

Per serving: 300 Calories; 17.5g Fat; 0.5g Carbs; 35.1g Protein; 0.1g Sugars; 0.4g Fiber

Ingredients

1 ½ pounds chuck eye steak

2 tablespoons olive oil

1 teaspoon paprika

1 tablespoon Dijon mustard

Kosher salt and ground black pepper, to taste

Directions

Toss the steak with the remaining ingredients; place the steak in the Air Fryer cooking basket.

Cook the steak at 400 degrees F for 12 minutes, turning it over halfway through the cooking time.

Bon appétit!

Roasted Short Loin

(Ready in about 15 minutes | Servings 5)

Per serving: 315 Calories; 14g Fat; 6.5g Carbs; 41.1g Protein; 5.1g Sugars; 0.2g Fiber

Ingredients

2 pounds short loin, sliced

2 tablespoons butter, room temperature

1 tablespoon dark brown sugar

1 teaspoon coarse sea salt

1 teaspoon ground black pepper

1 teaspoon cayenne pepper

1 teaspoon ground coriander

Directions

Toss the short loin with the remaining ingredients; place the short loin in the Air Fryer cooking basket.

Cook the short loin at 400 degrees F for 14 minutes, turning it over halfway through the cooking time.

Bon appétit!

Herb Butter London Broil

(Ready in about 30 minutes | Servings 4)
Per serving: 368 Calories; 29.5g Fat; 2.8g Carbs; 24.1g Protein; 0.9g Sugars; 0.5g Fiber
Ingredients
1 pound London broil
1/4 cup freshly squeezed lemon juice
1/4 cup olive oil
2 tablespoons tamari sauce
1 tablespoon stone-ground mustard
1 teaspoon mixed peppercorns, whole
3 tablespoons butter, cold
2 tablespoons fresh Italian herbs
1 teaspoon garlic powder
1/2 teaspoon kosher salt
Directions
Toss the beef with the lemon juice, olive oil, tamari sauce, mustard, and peppercorns; let it marinate for an hour.
Place the beef in a lightly oiled Air Fryer cooking basket and discard the marinade.
Cook the beef at 400 degrees F for 28 minutes, turning it over halfway through the cooking time.
Meanwhile, mix the butter, herbs, garlic powder, and salt. Serve warm beef with the chilled herb butter on the side.
Bon appétit!

Old-Fashioned Scotch Tender

(Ready in about 55 minutes | Servings 4)
Per serving: 339 Calories; 19.3g Fat; 4.8g Carbs; 36.4g Protein; 2.8g Sugars; 0.5g Fiber
Ingredients
1 ½ pounds Scotch tender
2 garlic cloves, pressed
1 tablespoon stone-ground mustard
2 tablespoons balsamic vinegar
2 tablespoons soy sauce
2 tablespoons olive oil
1 teaspoon garlic powder
Kosher salt and ground black pepper, to taste
Directions
Toss the Scotch tender with the remaining ingredients; place the Scotch tender in the Air Fryer cooking basket.
Cook the Scotch tender at 390 degrees F for 55 minutes, turning it over halfway through the cooking time.
Enjoy!

Hawaiian Roll Sliders

(Ready in about 20 minutes | Servings 4)

Per serving: 490 Calories; 17.3g Fat; 45g Carbs; 28.4g Protein; 4.6g Sugars; 6.5g Fiber

Ingredients

1 pound beef, ground

1 cup seasoned breadcrumbs

1 tablespoon fresh cilantro, finely chopped

1 tablespoon fresh parsley, finely chopped

8 Hawaiian butter dinner rolls

Directions

Mix all ingredients , except for the rolls. Shape the mixture into four patties.

Cook the burgers at 380 degrees F for about 15 minutes or until cooked through; make sure to turn them over halfway through the cooking time.

Serve your burgers on the prepared rolls and enjoy!

PORK

Apple and Madeira Glazed Ham

(Ready in about 1 hour | Servings 5)

Per serving: 359 Calories; 15.6g Fat; 23g Carbs; 30.3g Protein; 13.4g Sugars; 3.3g Fiber

Ingredients

2 pounds cooked ham
1 apple, cored and chopped
1/4 cup maple syrup
2 garlic cloves, crushed
1/4 cup Madeira wine

Directions

Start by preheating your Air Fryer to 400 degrees F for about 13 minutes.
In a mixing bowl, whisk all the remaining ingredients to make the glaze.
Wrap the ham in a piece of aluminum foil and lower it onto the Air Fryer cooking basket. Reduce the temperature to 375 degrees F and cook the ham for about 30 minutes.
Remove the foil, turn the temperature to 400 degrees F, and continue to cook an additional 15 minutes, coating the ham with the glaze every 5 minutes.
Bon appétit!

English Muffin Burgers

(Ready in about 20 minutes | Servings 4)

Per serving: 479 Calories; 48.1g Fat; 2.3g Carbs; 8.6g Protein; 1.6g Sugars; 0.1g Fiber

Ingredients

1 pound ground pork
1 egg
1/2 cup seasoned breadcrumbs
1 teaspoon dried oregano
1/2 teaspoon dried basil
Sea salt and ground black pepper, to taste
1 small red onion, chopped
1 teaspoon garlic, minced
1 tablespoon olive oil
4 English muffins

Directions

In a mixing bowl, thoroughly combine the pork, egg, breadcrumbs, spices, onion, garlic, and olive oil. Form the mixture into four patties.
Cook the burgers at 380 degrees F for about 15 minutes or until cooked through; make sure to turn them over halfway through the cooking time.
Serve your burgers with English muffins and enjoy!

Breaded Pork Cutlets

(Ready in about 20 minutes | Servings 4)

Per serving: 480 Calories; 25.1g Fat; 18.2g Carbs; 43.7g Protein; 0.9g Sugars; 1.4g Fiber

Ingredients

1 ½ pounds pork cutlets

Seasoned salt and ground black pepper, to taste

1 cup tortilla chips, crushed

1/2 teaspoon cayenne pepper

2 tablespoons olive oil

Directions

Toss the pork cutlets with the remaining ingredients; place them in a lightly oiled Air Fryer cooking basket.

Cook the pork cutlets at 400 degrees F for 15 minutes, turning them over halfway through the cooking time.

Bon appétit!

Bratwurst with Brussels Sprouts

(Ready in about 20 minutes | Servings 4)

Per serving: 438 Calories; 30.3g Fat; 25g Carbs; 18.7g Protein; 12g Sugars; 5.1g Fiber

Ingredients

1 pound bratwurst

1 pound Brussels sprouts

1 large onion, cut into wedges

1 teaspoon garlic, minced

1 tablespoon mustard

2 tablespoons honey

Directions

Toss all ingredients in a lightly greased Air Fryer cooking basket.

Air fry the sausage at 380 degrees F for approximately 15 minutes, tossing the basket halfway through the cooking time.

Bon appétit!

Dijon Pork Loin

(Ready in about 55 minutes | Servings 4)

Per serving: 302 Calories; 15.3g Fat; 1g Carbs; 36.9g Protein; 0g Sugars; 0.3g Fiber

Ingredients

1 ½ pounds pork top loin

1 tablespoon olive oil

1 tablespoon Dijon mustard

2 cloves garlic, crushed

1 tablespoon parsley

1 tablespoon coriander

1/2 teaspoon red pepper flakes, crushed

Kosher salt and ground black pepper, to taste

Directions

Toss all ingredients in a lightly greased Air Fryer cooking basket.

Cook the pork at 360 degrees F for 55 minutes, turning it over halfway through the cooking time.

Serve warm and enjoy!

Country-Style Ribs

(Ready in about 40 minutes | Servings 5)

Per serving: 371 Calories; 21.6g Fat; 4.4g Carbs; 35.4g Protein; 3.9g Sugars; 0.3g Fiber

Ingredients

2 pounds Country-style ribs

1/4 cup Sriracha sauce

2 tablespoons bourbon

1 tablespoon honey

1 teaspoon stone-ground mustard

Directions

Toss all ingredients in a lightly greased Air Fryer cooking basket.

Cook the pork ribs at 350 degrees F for 35 minutes, turning them over halfway through the cooking time.

Bon appétit!

Orange-Glazed Pork Chops

(Ready in about 20 minutes / Servings 3)

Per serving: 372 Calories; 22.5g Fat; 1.3g Carbs; 38.6g Protein; 1g Sugars; 0.2g Fiber

Ingredients

1 pound rib pork chops

1 ½ tablespoons butter, melted

2 tablespoons orange juice, freshly squeezed

1 teaspoon rosemary, chopped

Sea salt and cayenne pepper, to taste

Directions

Toss all ingredients in a lightly greased Air Fryer cooking basket.

Cook the pork chops at 400 degrees F for 15 minutes, turning them over halfway through the cooking time.

Bon appétit!

FISH & SEAFOOD

Chili Fried Calamari

(Ready in about 10 minutes / Servings 4)

Per serving: 316 Calories; 9.9g Fat; 30.1g Carbs; 24.4g Protein; 1.7g Sugars; 1.2g Fiber

Ingredients

1/2 cup milk

1 cup all-purpose flour

2 tablespoons olive oil

1 teaspoon turmeric powder

Sea salt flakes and ground black, to taste

1 teaspoon paprika

1 red chili, minced

1 pound calamari, cut into rings

Directions

In a mixing bowl, thoroughly combine the milk, flour, olive oil, turmeric powder, salt, black pepper, paprika, and red chili. Mix to combine well.

Now, dip your calamari into the flour mixture to coat.

Cook your calamari at 400 degrees F for 5 minutes, turning them over halfway through the cooking time.

Bon appétit!

Dad's Spicy Burgers

(Ready in about 15 minutes / Servings 4)

Per serving: 508 Calories; 23.7g Fat; 31.3g Carbs; 42.4g Protein; 2.4g Sugars; 2.6g Fiber

Ingredients

1 pound tilapia fish fillets, chopped

1/2 cup breadcrumbs

4 tablespoons shallots, chopped

2 garlic cloves, minced

1 tablespoon olive oil

8 dinner rolls

8 slices Provolone cheese

Directions

Mix all ingredients , except for the dinner rolls and cheese, in a bowl. Shape the mixture into four patties and place them in a lightly oiled Air Fryer cooking basket.

Cook the fish patties at 400 degrees F for about 14 minutes, turning them over halfway through the cooking time.

Serve with the cheese and dinner rolls. Enjoy!

Shrimp Salad Sandwich

(Ready in about 10 minutes | Servings 4)

Per serving: 422 Calories; 24.1g Fat; 23.2g Carbs; 27.5g Protein; 3.1g Sugars; 1.5g Fiber

Ingredients

1 pound shrimp, peeled and chilled
1 teaspoon olive oil
1 stalks celery, sliced
1 English cucumber, sliced
1 shallot, sliced
1 tablespoon fresh dill, roughly chopped
1 tablespoon fresh parsley, roughly chopped
1 tablespoon fresh lime juice
1 tablespoon apple cider vinegar
1/2 cup mayonnaise
1 teaspoon Creole seasoning mix
1 ½ teaspoons Dijon mustard
Coarse sea salt and lemon pepper, to taste
4 hoagie rolls

Directions

Toss the shrimp and olive oil in the Air Fryer cooking basket.

Cook the shrimp at 400 degrees F for 6 minutes, tossing the basket halfway through the cooking time.

Place the shrimp in a mixing bowl along with the remaining ingredients; toss to combine and serve on the prepared hoagie rolls.

Bon appétit!

Italian-Style Sea Bass

(Ready in about 15 minutes | Servings 4)

Per serving: 205 Calories; 10.5g Fat; 2.9g Carbs; 22.8g Protein; 0.8g Sugars; 0.7g Fiber

Ingredients

1 pound sea bass
2 garlic cloves, minced
2 tablespoons olive oil
1 tablespoon Italian seasoning mix
Sea salt and ground black pepper, to taste
1/4 cup dry white wine

Directions

Toss the fish with the remaining ingredients; place them in a lightly oiled Air Fryer cooking basket.

Cook the fish at 400 degrees F for about 10 minutes, turning them over halfway through the cooking time.

Bon appétit!

Fried Mustard Calamari

(Ready in about 10 minutes | Servings 4)

Per serving: 398 Calories; 9g Fat; 52g Carbs; 24.5g Protein; 0.8g Sugars; 2g Fiber

Ingredients

2 cups flour
Sea salt and ground black pepper, to taste
1 teaspoon garlic, minced
1 tablespoon mustard
2 tablespoons olive oil
1 pound calamari, sliced into rings

Directions

In a mixing bowl, thoroughly combine the flour, salt, black pepper, garlic, mustard, and, and olive oil. Mix to combine well.

Now, dip your calamari into the flour mixture to coat.

Cook your calamari at 400 degrees F for 5 minutes, turning them over halfway through the cooking time.

Bon appétit!

Italian Fish Fingers

(Ready in about 15 minutes | Servings 4)

Per serving: 218 Calories; 6.4g Fat; 14.6g Carbs; 23.8g Protein; 0.8g Sugars; 0.9g Fiber

Ingredients

1/2 cup all-purpose flour
Sea salt and ground black pepper
1 teaspoon cayenne pepper
1/2 teaspoon onion powder
1 tablespoon Italian parsley, chopped
1 teaspoon garlic powder
1 egg, whisked
1/2 cup Pecorino Romano cheese, grated
1 pound monkfish, sliced into strips

Directions

In a shallow bowl, mix the flour, spices, egg, and cheese. Dip the fish strips in the batter until they are well coated on all sides.

Arrange the fish strips in the Air Fryer cooking basket.

Cook the fish strips at 400 degrees F for about 10 minutes, shaking the basket halfway through the cooking time.

Bon appétit!

Spicy Fish Croquettes

(Ready in about 15 minutes | Servings 4)

Per serving: 258 Calories; 13.7g Fat; 11.3g Carbs; 18.8g Protein; 1.6g Sugars; 0.8g Fiber

Ingredients

1 pound catfish, skinless, boneless and chopped
2 tablespoons olive oil
2 cloves garlic, minced
1 small onion, minced
1/4 cup all-purpose flour
Sea salt and ground black pepper, to taste
1/2 cup breadcrumbs

Directions

Mix all ingredients in a bowl. Shape the mixture into bite-sized balls and place them in a lightly oiled Air Fryer cooking basket.

Cook the fish croquettes at 400 degrees F for about 14 minutes, shaking the basket halfway through the cooking time.

Bon appétit!

Southern-Style Shrimp

(Ready in about 15 minutes | Servings 4)

Per serving: 381 Calories; 1.4g Fat; 45.2g Carbs; 39.8g Protein; 5.2g Sugars; 5.4g Fiber

Ingredients

1 cup all-purpose flour
1 teaspoon Old Bay seasoning
Sea salt and lemon pepper, to taste
1/2 cup buttermilk
1 cup seasoned breadcrumbs
1 ½ pounds shrimp, peeled and deveined

Directions

In a shallow bowl, mix the flour, spices, and buttermilk. Place the seasoned breadcrumbs in the second bowl.
Dip the shrimp in the flour mixture, then in the breadcrumbs until they are well coated on all sides.
Arrange the shrimp in a well-greased Air Fryer cooking basket.
Cook the shrimp at 400 degrees F for about 10 minutes, shaking the basket halfway through the cooking time.
Bon appétit!

Mediterranean-Pita Wraps

(Ready in about 15 minutes | Servings 4)

Per serving: 366 Calories; 16.3g Fat; 16.4g Carbs; 38.1g Protein; 2.9g Sugars; 3.7g Fiber

Ingredients

1 pound mackerel fish fillets
2 tablespoons olive oil
1 tablespoon Mediterranean seasoning mix
1/2 teaspoon chili powder
Sea salt and freshly ground black pepper, to taste
2 ounces Feta cheese, crumbled
4 (6-1/2 inch) tortillas

Directions

Toss the fish fillets with the olive oil; place them in a lightly oiled Air Fryer cooking basket.
Cook the fish fillets at 400 degrees F for about 14 minutes, turning them over halfway through the cooking time.
Assemble your pitas with the chopped fish and remaining ingredients and serve warm. Bon appétit!

Butter Cilantro Shrimp

(Ready in about 10 minutes | Servings 4)

Per serving: 160 Calories; 6.3g Fat; 0.6g Carbs; 23.1g Protein; 0.1g Sugars; 0.2g Fiber

Ingredients

1 pound jumbo shrimp

2 tablespoons butter, at room temperature

Coarse sea salt and lemon pepper, to taste

2 tablespoons fresh cilantro, chopped

2 tablespoons fresh chives, chopped

2 garlic cloves, crushed

Directions

Toss all ingredients in a lightly greased Air Fryer cooking basket.

Cook the shrimp at 400 degrees F for 8 minutes, tossing the basket halfway through the cooking time.

Bon appétit!

Rosemary Sea Scallops

(Ready in about 10 minutes | Servings 4)

Per serving: 318 Calories; 15.1g Fat; 11.1g Carbs; 32.7g Protein; 0.6g Sugars; 0.4g Fiber

Ingredients

1 ½ pounds sea scallops

4 tablespoons butter, melted

1 tablespoon garlic, minced

Sea salt and ground black pepper, to season

2 rosemary sprigs, leaves picked and chopped

4 tablespoons dry white wine

Directions

Toss all ingredients in a lightly greased Air Fryer cooking basket.

Cook the scallops at 400 degrees F for 7 minutes, tossing the basket halfway through the cooking time.

Bon appétit!

Sausage-Stuffed Squid

(Ready in about 10 minutes | Servings 4)

Per serving: 280 Calories; 13.7g Fat; 11.2g Carbs; 26.3g Protein; 1.8g Sugars; 1.5g Fiber

Ingredients

2 tablespoons olive oil, divided, or as needed
1 small onion, chopped
2 cloves garlic, minced
1 tablespoon fresh parsley, chopped
1 small Italian pepper, chopped
Sea salt and ground black pepper, to taste
4 ounces beef sausage, crumbled
1 pound squid tubes, cleaned

Directions

In a mixing bowl, thoroughly combine the olive oil, onion, garlic, parsley, Italian pepper, salt, black pepper, and sausage.

Stuff the squid tubes with the sausage filling and secure them with toothpicks. Place them in a lightly oiled Air Fryer cooking basket.

Cook the stuffed squid tubes at 400 degrees F for 5 minutes, turning them over halfway through the cooking time.

Bon appétit!

Perfect Haddock Fishcakes

(Ready in about 15 minutes | Servings 4)

Per serving: 400 Calories; 11.7g Fat; 39g Carbs; 33.3g Protein; 3.8g Sugars; 1.7g Fiber

Ingredients

1 pound haddock, boneless and
1/4 cup all-purpose flour
2 eggs
1/2 cup parmesan cheese, grated
1/2 cup breadcrumbs
4 brioche buns

Directions

Mix all ingredients, except for the brioche buns, in a bowl. Shape the mixture into four patties and place them in a lightly oiled Air Fryer cooking basket.

Cook the fish patties at 400 degrees F for about 14 minutes, turning them over halfway through the cooking time.

Serve on hamburger buns and enjoy!

Creamed Shrimp Salad

(Ready in about 10 minutes | Servings 4)

Per serving: 282 Calories; 14.1g Fat; 3g Carbs; 36.3g Protein; 1.1g Sugars; 1g Fiber

Ingredients

1 ½ pounds shrimp, peeled and deveined
1 tablespoon olive oil
Sea salt and freshly ground black pepper, to taste
1 teaspoon fresh dill, chopped
1 teaspoon fresh basil, chopped
1 tablespoon fresh parsley, chopped
2 tablespoons chives, chopped
1 bell pepper, seeded and chopped
1 celery stalk, trimmed and chopped
1/2 cup mayonnaise
1 teaspoon stone-ground mustard
1 tablespoon fresh lime juice

Directions

Toss the shrimp and olive oil in the Air Fryer cooking basket.
Cook the shrimp at 400 degrees F for 6 minutes, tossing the basket halfway through the cooking time.
Place the shrimp in a salad bowl; add in the remaining ingredients and gently stir to combine.
Serve well-chilled.
Bon appétit!

Mediterranean Herb Calamari (Kalamarakia Tiganita)

(Ready in about 10 minutes | Servings 4)

Per serving: 293 Calories; 15.3g Fat; 19.2g Carbs; 19.1g Protein; 2g Sugars; 1g Fiber

Ingredients

1 pound calamari, sliced into rings
Sea salt and ground black pepper, to taste
1 teaspoon cayenne pepper
1 teaspoon garlic powder
2 tablespoons lemon juice
2 tablespoons olive oil

Directions

Toss all ingredients in a lightly greased Air Fryer cooking basket.
Cook your calamari at 400 degrees F for 5 minutes, tossing the basket halfway through the cooking time.
Bon appétit!

Sea Scallop Salad

(Ready in about 10 minutes | Servings 4)

Per serving: 243 Calories; 10.2g Fat; 3.3g Carbs; 32.1g Protein; 1.8g Sugars; 0.5g Fiber

Ingredients

1 ½ pounds sea scallops
Sea salt and ground black pepper, to taste
2 tablespoons olive oil
1 tablespoon balsamic vinegar
2 garlic cloves, minced
2 teaspoons fresh tarragon, minced
1 teaspoon Dijon mustard
1 cup mixed baby greens
1 small tomato, diced

Directions

Toss the scallops, salt, and black pepper in a lightly greased Air Fryer cooking basket.

Cook the scallops at 400 degrees F for 7 minutes, tossing the basket halfway through the cooking time.

Toss the scallops with the remaining ingredients and serve at room temperature or well-chilled. Bon appétit!

Classic Fish Burgers

(Ready in about 15 minutes | Servings 4)

Per serving: 368 Calories; 20.7g Fat; 23.3g Carbs; 20.9g Protein; 3.4g Sugars; 1.4g Fiber

Ingredients

1 pound halibut, chopped
2 garlic cloves, crushed
4 tablespoons scallions, chopped
Sea salt and ground black pepper, to taste
1 teaspoon smoked paprika
A pinch of grated nutmeg
1 tablespoon olive oil
4 hamburger buns

Directions

Mix all ingredients , except for the hamburger buns, in a bowl. Shape the mixture into four patties and place them in a lightly oiled Air Fryer cooking basket.

Cook the fish patties at 400 degrees F for about 14 minutes, turning them over halfway through the cooking time.

Serve on hamburger buns and enjoy!

Decadent Coconut Shrimp

(Ready in about 10 minutes | Servings 4)

Per serving: 366 Calories; 16.3g Fat; 16.4g Carbs; 38.1g Protein; 2.9g Sugars; 3.7g Fiber

Ingredients

1/2 cup whole wheat flour
1 cup coconut, shredded
1/4 cup buttermilk
2 tablespoons olive oil
2 garlic cloves, crushed
1 tablespoon fresh lemon juice
Sea salt and red pepper flakes, to taste
1 ½ pounds shrimp, peeled and deveined

Directions

Mix the flour, coconut, buttermilk, olive oil, garlic, lemon juice, salt, and red pepper in a mixing bowl.

Dip the shrimp in the batter and place them in a well-greased Air Fryer cooking basket.

Cook the shrimp at 400 degrees F for 9 minutes, tossing the basket halfway through the cooking time.

Bon appétit!

Tuna Salad with a Twist

(Ready in about 15 minutes | Servings 4)

Per serving: 187 Calories; 5.7g Fat; 5.3g Carbs; 27.5g Protein; 2.3g Sugars; 1.3g Fiber

Ingredients

1 pound fresh tuna steak
Sea salt and ground black pepper, to taste
2 tablespoons fresh lemon juice
1 small onion, thinly sliced
1 carrot, julienned
2 cups baby spinach
2 tablespoons parsley, roughly chopped

Directions

Toss the fish with the salt and black pepper; place your tuna in a lightly oiled Air Fryer cooking basket.

Cook your tuna at 400 degrees F for about 10 minutes, turning it over halfway through the cooking time.

Chop your tuna with two forks and add in the remaining ingredients; stir to combine and serve well-chilled.

Bon appétit!

Tangy Butter Scallops

(Ready in about 10 minutes | Servings 4)

Per serving: 157 Calories; 7.8g Fat; 5.8g Carbs; 15.4g Protein; 0.8g Sugars; 0.2g Fiber

Ingredients

1 pound sea scallops

2 tablespoons butter, room temperature

2 tablespoons lemon juice

2 garlic cloves, crushed

Salt and fresh ground black pepper to taste

1/4 cup dry white wine

Directions

Toss all ingredients in a lightly greased Air Fryer cooking basket.

Cook the scallops at 400 degrees F for 7 minutes, tossing the basket halfway through the cooking time.

Bon appétit!

Lobster with Butter and Spring Onions

(Ready in about 10 minutes | Servings 4)

Per serving: 199 Calories; 12.4g Fat; 2.3g Carbs; 19.3g Protein; 0.8g Sugars; 0.4g Fiber

Ingredients

1 pound lobster tails

4 tablespoons butter, room temperature

2 garlic cloves, minced

Coarse sea salt and freshly cracked black pepper, to taste

4 tablespoons springs onions

1 tablespoon fresh lime juice

Directions

Butterfly the lobster tails by cutting through the shell and place them in a lightly oiled Air Fryer basket.

In a mixing bowl, thoroughly combine the remaining ingredients.

Now, spread 1/2 of the butter mixture over the top of the lobster meat. Air fry the lobster tails at 380 degrees F for 4 minutes.

After that, spread another 1/2 of the butter mixture on top; continue to cook for a further 4 minutes.

Bon appétit!

Butter and Parsley Calamari

(Ready in about 10 minutes | Servings 4)

Per serving: 263 Calories; 8.9g Fat; 7.8g Carbs; 35.4g Protein; 0.1g Sugars; 0.2g Fiber

Ingredients

1 pound calamari, sliced into rings
2 tablespoons butter
2 tablespoons parsley, chopped
2 garlic cloves, minced
1 teaspoon cayenne pepper
Sea salt and freshly ground black pepper, to taste

Directions

Toss all ingredients in a lightly greased Air Fryer cooking basket.
Cook your calamari at 400 degrees F for 5 minutes, tossing the basket halfway through the cooking time.
Bon appétit!

RICE & GRAINS

Hot and Spicy Mac and Cheese

(Ready in about 20 minutes | Servings 4)
Per serving: 293 Calories; 11.3g Fat; 26.7g Carbs; 21.2g Protein; 2g Sugars; 2.3g Fiber
Ingredients
1 cups macaroni
1 cup cream of onion soup
2 tablespoons butter
4 ounces Ricotta cheese
6 ounces mozzarella cheese, crumbled
Kosher salt and ground white pepper, to taste
1/2 teaspoon cumin, ground
1 teaspoon dry mustard
1 teaspoon red chili powder
Directions
Cook the macaroni according to the package directions.
Drain the macaroni and place them in a lightly greased baking pan.
Fold in the remaining ingredients and stir to combine.
Bake your mac and cheese in the preheated Air Fryer at 360 degrees F for about 15 minutes.
Serve garnished with fresh Italian herbs, if desired.
Bon appétit!

Blueberry Crescent Rolls

(Ready in about 15 minutes | Servings 6)
Per serving: 343 Calories; 16.3g Fat; 44.3g Carbs; 5.6g Protein; 29g Sugars; 1.6g Fiber
Ingredients
1 (8-ounce) can refrigerated crescent dinner rolls
6 ounces cream cheese, room temperature
4 tablespoons granulated sugar
1 teaspoon lemon zest, grated
1 cup fresh blueberries
1 cup powdered sugar
1/4 teaspoon ground cinnamon
Directions
Separate the dough into rectangles. Mix the remaining ingredients until well combined.
Spread each rectangle with the cheese mixture; roll them up tightly.
Place the rolls in the Air Fryer cooking basket.
Bake the rolls at 300 degrees F for about 5 minutes; turn them over and bake for a further 5 minutes.
Bon appétit!

Decadent Porridge with Apricots

(Ready in about 15 minutes | Servings 4)

Per serving: 407 Calories; 13.4g Fat; 66g Carbs; 7.4g Protein; 29.1g Sugars; 5.2g Fiber

Ingredients

1/2 cup old fashioned oats
1/2 cup quinoa flakes
1/4 cup almonds, chopped
1/4 cup pecans, chopped
2 cups orange juice
4 tablespoons honey
2 tablespoons coconut oil
4 tablespoons dried apricots, chopped

Directions

Thoroughly combine all ingredients in a mixing bowl. Spoon the mixture into lightly greased mugs.

Then, place the mugs in the Air Fryer cooking basket. Bake your porridge at 380 degrees F for about 12 minutes.

Serve immediately. Bon appétit!

Greek-Style Muffins

(Ready in about 20 minutes | Servings 6)

Per serving: 172 Calories; 1.2g Fat; 35.1g Carbs; 5.1g Protein; 15.4g Sugars; 1.6g Fiber

Ingredients

1 cup all-purpose flour
1 teaspoon baking powder
1/2 brown sugar
1 Greek yogurt
1/2 cup prunes, pitted and chopped
1 egg, beaten
1 teaspoon vanilla essence

Directions

Start by preheating your Air Fryer to 330 degrees F.

Mix all ingredients until well-combined; then, divide the batter evenly between silicone baking molds; place them in the Air Fryer cooking basket.

Bake your muffins for about 15 minutes or until a tester comes out dry and clean.

Allow the muffins to cool before unmolding and serving. Bon appétit!

Perfect Indian Biryani

(Ready in about 15 minutes | Servings 4)
Per serving: 188 Calories; 6.6g Fat; 24.1g Carbs; 2.9g Protein; 0.7g Sugars; 2.1g Fiber
Ingredients
2 cups jasmine rice, cooked
1 cup water
1 teaspoon ginger-garlic paste
2 tablespoons shallots, chopped
1/2 teaspoon ground cinnamon
2 tablespoons butter
1/2 teaspoon cumin seeds
1 teaspoon garam masala
1/2 teaspoon turmeric powder
Directions
Start by preheating your Air Fryer to 360 degrees F.
Thoroughly combine all ingredients in a lightly greased baking pan.
Lower the pan into the Air Fryer cooking basket. Cook for about 10 minutes or until cooked through.
Bon appétit!

Autumn Oatmeal Cups

(Ready in about 20 minutes | Servings 4)
Per serving: 412 Calories; 13.9g Fat; 64.1g Carbs; 11.1g Protein; 33g Sugars; 6.2g Fiber
Ingredients
1 cup full-fat milk
1 cup applesauce, unsweetened
1 egg, beaten
1/2 cup pure maple syrup
1 cup old-fashioned oats
1 teaspoon baking powder
1 teaspoon pure vanilla extract
1/2 teaspoon ground cinnamon
1/4 teaspoon freshly grated nutmeg
A pinch of kosher salt
1/2 cup pecans, chopped
Directions
Thoroughly combine all ingredients in a mixing bowl. Spoon the mixture into lightly greased mugs.
Then, place the mugs in the Air Fryer cooking basket. Bake your oatmeal at 380 degrees F for about 12 minutes.
Bon appétit!

Grandma's Pumpkin Porridge

(Ready in about 15 minutes | Servings 5)

Per serving: 412 Calories; 13.9g Fat; 64.1g Carbs; 11.1g Protein; 33g Sugars; 6.2g Fiber

Ingredients

1/2 cup old-fashioned oats
1/2 cup quinoa flakes
1/4 cup pecans, chopped
2 tablespoons chia seeds, ground
2 tablespoons flax seeds, ground
1 teaspoon vanilla essence
2 ounces dark chocolate chips
1/2 cup canned pumpkin
1/2 cup almond milk

Directions

Thoroughly combine all ingredients in a mixing bowl. Spoon the mixture into a lightly greased baking pan.

Then, place the baking pan in the Air Fryer cooking basket. Bake your porridge at 380 degrees F for about 12 minutes.

Serve immediately. Bon appétit!

Aromatic Rice Pudding

(Ready in about 20 minutes | Servings 4)

Per serving: 319 Calories; 10.7g Fat; 51.8g Carbs; 5.6g Protein; 30g Sugars; 2.4g Fiber

Ingredients

2 cups brown rice, cooked
1 ½ cups coconut milk
1/4 cup agave syrup
1 teaspoon vanilla
2 tablespoons coconut oil
2 tablespoons rose water
4 tablespoons dried apricots, chopped
A pinch of sea salt

Directions

Thoroughly combine all ingredients in a lightly greased baking pan.

Lower the pan into the Air Fryer cooking basket. Cook for about 15 minutes or until cooked through.

Bon appétit!

Traditional Chawal ke Pakore

(Ready in about 20 minutes / Servings 4)

Per serving: 268 Calories; 11.5g Fat; 34.4g Carbs; 6.6g Protein; 0.8g Sugars; 1.5g Fiber

Ingredients

1 cup rice flour

1/2 onion, chopped

2 garlic cloves, minced

2 tablespoons butter, room temperature

1 teaspoon paprika

1 teaspoon cumin powder

1/2 cup Paneer cheese, crumbled

Directions

Start by preheating your Air Fryer to 380 degrees F.

Mix all ingredients until everything is well combined. Form the mixture into patties.

Air fry the patties for about 15 minutes or until cooked through. Turn them over halfway through the cooking time.

Bon appétit!

Cheesy Rice Casserole

(Ready in about 15 minutes / Servings 4)

Per serving: 332 Calories; 14.1g Fat; 38.1g Carbs; 12g Protein; 7.4g Sugars; 2.9g Fiber

Ingredients

1 small shallot, minced

2 garlic cloves, minced

2 tablespoons olive oil

1/2 teaspoon paprika

2 eggs, whisked

1 cup half-and-half

1 cup cheddar cheese, shredded

2 cups cooked brown rice

1 tablespoon Italian parsley leaves, chopped

1 cup cream of celery soup

Sea salt and freshly ground black pepper, to taste

Directions

Start by preheating your Air Fryer to 360 degrees F.

Thoroughly combine all ingredients in a lightly greased baking pan. Lower the pan into the Air Fryer cooking basket.

Cook for about 10 minutes or until cooked through.

Bon appétit!

Bourbon Vanilla French Toast

(Ready in about 15 minutes | Servings 4)

Per serving: 188 Calories; 12.7g Fat; 11.4g Carbs; 6.7g Protein; 2.4g Sugars; 0.7g Fiber

Ingredients

2 eggs, beaten

1/4 cup milk

2 tablespoons coconut oil, room temperature

1/2 teaspoon bourbon vanilla extract

1/2 teaspoon ground cinnamon

4 slices bread

Directions

In a mixing bowl, thoroughly combine the eggs, milk, coconut oil, vanilla, and cinnamon.

Then dip each piece of bread into the egg mixture; place the bread slices in a lightly greased baking pan.

Air Fryer the bread slices at 330 degrees F for about 4 minutes; turn them over and cook for a further 3 to 4 minutes. Enjoy!

Mini Monkey Breads

(Ready in about 15 minutes | Servings 5)

Per serving: 322 Calories; 16.1g Fat; 38.9g Carbs; 5.6g Protein; 21g Sugars; 2.1g Fiber

Ingredients

1 (8-ounces) can crescent rolls

1 teaspoon ground cinnamon

4 ounces cream cheese, room temperature

1/4 cup sugar

2 tablespoons full-fat milk

1/2 cup apple pie filling, canned

Directions

Separate the dough into rectangles. Mix the remaining ingredients until well combined.

Spread each rectangle with the cinnamon/cheese mixture; roll them up tightly.

Place the rolls in the Air Fryer cooking basket.

Bake the rolls at 300 degrees F for about 5 minutes; turn them over and bake for a further 5 minutes.

Bon appétit!

Traditional Chinese Rice

(Ready in about 15 minutes | Servings 4)

Per serving: 252 Calories; 10.5g Fat; 32.1g Carbs; 6.8g Protein; 4.4g Sugars; 4.8g Fiber

Ingredients

2 cups multigrain rice, cooked
1 small onion, finely chopped
1 teaspoon garlic, minced
2 tablespoons sesame oil
1 egg, whisked
2 tablespoons soy sauce
1 carrot, chopped
1 cup green peas
Sea salt and red chili flakes, to taste

Directions

Start by preheating your Air Fryer to 360 degrees F.

Thoroughly combine all ingredients in a lightly greased baking pan.

Lower the pan into the Air Fryer cooking basket. Cook for about 10 minutes or until cooked through.

Bon appétit!

Breakfast Mocha Muffins

(Ready in about 20 minutes | Servings 6)

Per serving: 189 Calories; 5.3g Fat; 32.6g Carbs; 5.1g Protein; 19.4g Sugars; 3.1g Fiber

Ingredients

1/2 cup coconut flour
1/2 cup all-purpose flour
1/2 cup cocoa powder
1/2 cup brown sugar
1/2 teaspoon baking powder
A pinch of sea salt
A pinch of grated nutmeg
1 tablespoon instant coffee granules
1/2 cup milk
2 eggs, whisked
1/2 teaspoon vanilla extract

Directions

Start by preheating your Air Fryer to 330 degrees F.

Mix all ingredients until well-combined; then, divide the batter evenly between silicone baking molds; place them in the Air Fryer cooking basket.

Bake your muffins for about 15 minutes or until a tester comes out dry and clean.

Allow the muffins to cool before unmolding and serving. Bon appétit!

Porridge with Sultanas

(Ready in about 15 minutes | Servings 5)

Per serving: 263 Calories; 12.3g Fat; 30.3g Carbs; 8.6g Protein; 5.1g Sugars; 3.7g Fiber

Ingredients

1/2 cup old-fashioned oats
1/2 cup millet, rinsed and drained
2 tablespoons flax seeds, ground
1/2 cup Sultanas
2 cups coconut milk
2 tablespoons coconut oil
A pinch of salt
A pinch of ground cloves

Directions

Thoroughly combine all ingredients in a mixing bowl. Spoon the mixture into a lightly greased baking pan.

Then, place the baking pan in the Air Fryer cooking basket. Bake your porridge at 380 degrees F for about 12 minutes.

Serve immediately. Bon appétit!

Easy Chia Oatmeal

(Ready in about 15 minutes | Servings 4)

Per serving: 315 Calories; 6.3g Fat; 57g Carbs; 9.6g Protein; 28.4g Sugars; 6.5g Fiber

Ingredients

1 cup old-fashioned oats
1 teaspoon baking powder
1/2 teaspoon cinnamon
A pinch of sea salt
A pinch of grated nutmeg
1 cup coconut milk
1 cup pineapple juice
1/4 cup agave syrup
2 tablespoons ground chia seeds
1 teaspoon vanilla extract

Directions

Thoroughly combine all ingredients in a mixing bowl. Spoon the mixture into lightly greased mugs.

Then, place the mugs in the Air Fryer cooking basket. Bake your oatmeal at 380 degrees F for about 12 minutes.

Bon appétit!

Brioche Pudding with A Twist

(Ready in about 35 minutes | Servings 6)

Per serving: 219 Calories; 13.3g Fat; 16.7g Carbs; 7.5g Protein; 9.8g Sugars; 1.5g Fiber

Ingredients

2 cups Brioche bread, cubed
1/2 teaspoon cinnamon powder
4 tablespoons brown sugar
2 eggs, whisked
2 tablespoons coconut oil
1 cup eggnog
1/2 cup almonds, chopped

Directions

Place the bread cubes in a lightly greased baking pan.
In a mixing bowl, thoroughly combine the remaining ingredients.
Pour the custard mixture over the bread cubes. Set aside for 15 minutes to soak.
Bake the bread pudding at 350 degrees F for about 20 minutes or until the custard is set but still a little wobbly.
Bon appétit!

Traditional Indian Bhajji

(Ready in about 20 minutes | Servings 4)

Per serving: 238 Calories; 7.1g Fat; 38.4g Carbs; 5g Protein; 1.8g Sugars; 2.5g Fiber

Ingredients

1 cup rice flour
4 tablespoons chickpea flour
1/2 teaspoon sweet paprika
1 teaspoon chili powder
Sea salt and ground black pepper, to taste
1/2 cup green cabbage, shredded
1 teaspoon onion powder
1 teaspoon garlic powder
2 tablespoons butter
1/2 cup vegetable broth

Directions

Start by preheating your Air Fryer to 380 degrees F.
Mix all ingredients until everything is well combined. Form the mixture into patties.
Air fry the patties for about 15 minutes or until cooked through. Turn them over halfway through the cooking time.
Bon appétit!

Mediterranean-Style Biscuits

(Ready in about 20 minutes | Servings 6)

Per serving: 180 Calories; 9.2g Fat; 18.8g Carbs; 2.7g Protein; 0.1g Sugars; 0.6g Fiber

Ingredients

1 cup all-purpose flour
1 teaspoon baking powder
4 tablespoons olive oil
1/2 cup sour cream
A pinch of sea salt
1 teaspoon Mediterranean seasoning mix

Directions

Start by preheating your Air Fryer to 360 degrees F.

Mix all ingredients until well combined. Use a 2-inch biscuit cutter and cut out biscuits. Place the biscuits on a lightly greased baking pan.

Lower the pan into the Air Fryer basket.

Bake your biscuits for about 15 minutes or until a tester comes out dry and clean. Bon appétit!

Easy Rice Pudding

(Ready in about 20 minutes | Servings 4)

Per serving: 218 Calories; 5.2g Fat; 35.6g Carbs; 6.7g Protein; 22.1g Sugars; 1.4g Fiber

Ingredients

1 cup pudding rice
3 tablespoons honey
2 cups milk
1 cup half-and-half
1 teaspoon vanilla extract
1/2 teaspoon ground cinnamon

Directions

Thoroughly combine all ingredients in a lightly greased baking pan.

Lower the pan into the Air Fryer cooking basket. Cook for about 15 minutes or until cooked through.

Bon appétit!

Cornbread French Toast Casserole

(Ready in about 20 minutes | Servings 6)

Per serving: 268 Calories; 14.5g Fat; 26g Carbs; 5.8g Protein; 11g Sugars; 0.8g Fiber

Ingredients

3 eggs
2 tablespoons coconut oil, room temperature
1/2 cup heavy cream
1 teaspoon vanilla
1/2 cup brown sugar
1/2 teaspoon ground cinnamon
A pinch of grated nutmeg
A pinch of salt
6 slices sweet cornbread

Directions

In a mixing bowl, thoroughly combine the eggs, coconut oil, heavy cream, vanilla, sugar, cinnamon, nutmeg, and salt.

Then, place the cornbread slices in a lightly greased baking pan. Pour the custard mixture over the cornbread slices.

Bake your casserole at 330 degrees F for about 12 minutes. Enjoy!

Risotto ala Carbonara

(Ready in about 15 minutes | Servings 4)

Per serving: 430 Calories; 31.2g Fat; 27.2g Carbs; 10.1g Protein; 1.3g Sugars; 1.9g Fiber

Ingredients

2 cups Arborio rice, cooked
2 tablespoons sesame oil
1 shallot, chopped
1/2 cup white Italian wine
1/2 cup heavy cream
Coarse sea salt and freshly ground black pepper, to taste
4 tablespoons pancetta, chopped
1 cup Parmesan cheese, preferably freshly grated
1 tablespoon fresh Italian parsley, chopped

Directions

Start by preheating your Air Fryer to 360 degrees F.

Thoroughly combine all ingredients in a lightly greased baking pan.

Lower the pan into the Air Fryer cooking basket. Cook for about 10 minutes or until cooked through.

Bon appétit!

Three-Grain Porridge

(Ready in about 15 minutes | Servings 5)

Per serving: 336 Calories; 6.3g Fat; 63.1g Carbs; 12.3g Protein; 20.7g Sugars; 6.6g Fiber

Ingredients

1/2 cup rolled oats
1/2 cup quinoa flakes
1/2 cup rye flakes
1 cup coconut milk
1 cup orange juice
2 eggs, whisked
4 tablespoons honey
1/2 teaspoon ground cinnamon

Directions

Thoroughly combine all ingredients in a mixing bowl. Spoon the mixture into a lightly greased baking pan.

Then, place the baking pan in the Air Fryer cooking basket. Bake your porridge at 380 degrees F for about 12 minutes.

Serve immediately. Bon appétit!

Cheesy Cornbread Muffins

(Ready in about 25 minutes | Servings 4)

Per serving: 319 Calories; 18.2g Fat; 32.1g Carbs; 7.9g Protein; 1.7g Sugars; 2.6g Fiber

Ingredients

1 cup self-rising cornmeal
4 ounces canned creamed corn
1/2 cup Colby cheese, shredded
1/4 cup milk
1/4 cup butter, room temperature

Directions

Start by preheating your Air Fryer to 360 degrees F.

Mix all ingredients until everything is well incorporated. Scrape the batter into baking molds and place them in the Air Fryer basket.

Bake your cornbread muffins for about 22 minutes or until a tester comes out dry and clean.

Allow your cornbread muffins to cool before unmolding and serving. Bon appétit!

SNACKS & APPETIZERS

Spicy Spare Ribs

(Ready in about 40 minutes | Servings 4)

Per serving: 442 Calories; 33g Fat; 4.7g Carbs; 32.3g Protein; 1.9g Sugars; 0.5g Fiber

Ingredients

1 ½ pounds spare ribs

Kosher salt and ground black pepper, to taste

2 teaspoons brown sugar

1 teaspoon paprika

1 teaspoon chile powder

1 teaspoon garlic powder

Directions

Toss all the ingredients in a lightly greased Air Fryer cooking basket.

Cook the pork ribs at 350 degrees F for 35 minutes, turning them over halfway through the cooking time.

Bon appétit!

Butter Roasted Baby Carrots

(Ready in about 20 minutes | Servings 4)

Per serving: 104 Calories; 6.3g Fat; 12.4g Carbs; 1.8g Protein; 6g Sugars; 3.7g Fiber

Ingredients

1 pound baby carrots

2 tablespoons butter

Kosher salt and ground white pepper, to taste

1 teaspoon paprika

1 teaspoon dried oregano

Directions

Toss the carrots with the remaining ingredients; then, arrange the carrots in the Air Fryer cooking basket.

Cook the carrots at 380 degrees F for 15 minutes, shaking the basket halfway through the cooking time.

Bon appétit!

Sticky Chicken Wings

(Ready in about 20 minutes | Servings 5)

Per serving: 344 Calories; 13g Fat; 15.3g Carbs; 40.5g Protein; 14.4g Sugars; 1g Fiber

Ingredients

2 pounds chicken wings
1/4 cup agave syrup
2 tablespoons soy sauce
2 tablespoons scallions, chopped
2 tablespoons olive oil
1 teaspoon ginger, peeled and grated
2 cloves garlic, minced
Sea salt and ground black pepper, to taste

Directions

Toss the chicken wings with the remaining ingredients.

Cook the chicken wings at 380 degrees F for 18 minutes, turning them over halfway through the cooking time.

Bon appétit!

Classic Yam Chips

(Ready in about 20 minutes | Servings 2)

Per serving: 141 Calories; 6.6g Fat; 20.5g Carbs; 1.5g Protein; 0.3g Sugars; 3.1g Fiber

Ingredients

1 large-sized yam, peeled and cut into 1/4-inch sticks
1 tablespoon olive oil
Kosher salt and red pepper, to taste

Directions

Start by preheating your Air Fryer to 360 degrees F.

Toss the yam with the remaining ingredients and place them in the Air Fryer cooking basket.

Air fry the yam sticks for 15 minutes, tossing halfway through the cooking time and working in batches.

Enjoy!

Potato Chips with a Twist

(Ready in about 20 minutes | Servings 3)

Per serving: 281 Calories; 10.1g Fat; 43.5g Carbs; 1.5g Protein; 1.9g Sugars; 5.1g Fiber

Ingredients

2 large-sized potatoes, peeled and thinly sliced
2 tablespoons olive oil
1 teaspoon Sichuan peppercorns
1 teaspoon garlic powder
1/2 teaspoon Chinese five-spice powder
Sea salt, to taste

Directions

Start by preheating your Air Fryer to 360 degrees F.
Toss the potatoes with the remaining ingredients and place them in the Air Fryer cooking basket.
Air fry the potato chips for 16 minutes, shaking the basket halfway through the cooking time and working in batches.
Enjoy!

Crispy Zucchini Fries

(Ready in about 15 minutes | Servings 4)

Per serving: 281 Calories; 10.1g Fat; 43.5g Carbs; 1.5g Protein; 1.9g Sugars; 5.1g Fiber

Ingredients

1 pound zucchini, cut into sticks
1 egg, whisked
1/4 cup parmesan cheese, grated
1/2 cup breadcrumbs
1 teaspoon garlic powder
1/2 teaspoon onion powder
Sea salt and ground black pepper, to taste

Directions

Start by preheating your Air Fryer to 390 degrees F.
Toss the zucchini sticks with the remaining ingredients and arrange them in a single layer in the Air Fryer cooking basket.
Cook the zucchini sticks for about 10 minutes at 390 degrees F, shaking the basket halfway through the cooking time. Work in batches.
Bon appétit!

Sriracha Chicken Wings

(Ready in about 20 minutes | Servings 4)

Per serving: 403 Calories; 19.4g Fat; 3.3g Carbs; 50.1g Protein; 1.3g Sugars; 0.7g Fiber

Ingredients

2 pounds chicken wings
1 tablespoon white vinegar
Sea salt and ground black pepper, to taste
1 teaspoon cayenne pepper
1 teaspoon garlic powder
1/2 teaspoon onion powder
4 tablespoons butter, room temperature
1/4 cup Sriracha sauce

Directions

Toss the chicken wings with the remaining ingredients.
Cook the chicken wings at 380 degrees F for 18 minutes, turning them over halfway through the cooking time.
Bon appétit!

Wax Bean Fries

(Ready in about 10 minutes | Servings 4)

Per serving: 69 Calories; 2.4g Fat; 8.7g Carbs; 2.2g Protein; 3.7g Sugars; 3.2g Fiber

Ingredients

1 pound fresh wax beans, trimmed
2 teaspoons olive oil
1/2 teaspoon onion powder
1 teaspoon garlic powder
1/2 teaspoon cumin powder
Sea salt and ground black pepper, to taste

Directions

Toss the wax beans with the remaining ingredients.
Air fry the wax beans at 390 degrees F for about 6 minutes, tossing the basket halfway through the cooking time.
Enjoy!

Balsamic Eggplant Fries

(Ready in about 20 minutes | Servings 3)

Per serving: 124 Calories; 9.2g Fat; 10.1g Carbs; 1.5g Protein; 6.4g Sugars; 3.8g Fiber

Ingredients

3/4 pound eggplant

Sea salt and ground black pepper, to taste

1/2 teaspoon paprika

2 tablespoons olive oil

2 tablespoons balsamic vinegar

Directions

Toss the eggplant pieces with the remaining ingredients until they are well coated on all sides.

Arrange the eggplant in the Air Fryer basket.

Cook the eggplant at 400 degrees F for about 15 minutes, shaking the basket halfway through the cooking time.

Bon appétit!

Cheesy Tomato Chips

(Ready in about 20 minutes | Servings 3)

Per serving: 154 Calories; 13.3g Fat; 5.1g Carbs; 4.1g Protein; 3.1g Sugars; 1g Fiber

Ingredients

1 large-sized beefsteak tomatoes

2 tablespoons olive oil

1/2 teaspoon paprika

Sea salt, to taste

1 teaspoon garlic powder

1 tablespoon fresh cilantro, chopped

4 tablespoons Pecorino cheese, grated

Directions

Toss the tomato slices with the olive oil and spices until they are well coated on all sides.

Arrange the tomato slices in the Air Fryer cooking basket.

Cook the tomato slices at 360 degrees F for about 10 minutes. Turn the temperature to 330 degrees F and top the tomato slices with the cheese; now, continue to cook for a further 5 minutes.

Bon appétit!

Hot Spicy Nuts

(Ready in about 10 minutes | Servings 4)

Per serving: 264 Calories; 24.3g Fat; 8.8g Carbs; 7.6g Protein; 2.2g Sugars; 4.7g Fiber

Ingredients

1 egg white lightly beaten
1/2 cup pecan halves
1/2 cup almonds
1/2 cup walnuts
Sea salt and cayenne pepper, to taste
1 teaspoon chili powder
1/2 teaspoon ground cinnamon
1/2 teaspoon ground allspice

Directions

Preheat your Air Fryer to 330 degrees F.
Mix the nuts with the rest of the ingredients and place them in the Air Fryer cooking basket.
Air fry the nuts for 6 minutes, shaking the basket halfway through the cooking time and working in batches.
Enjoy!

Golden Beet Chips

(Ready in about 35 minutes | Servings 2)

Per serving: 188 Calories; 13.6g Fat; 15.1g Carbs; 2.7g Protein; 9g Sugars; 4.2g Fiber

Ingredients

1/2 pound golden beets, peeled and thinly sliced
Kosher salt and ground black pepper, to taste
1 teaspoon paprika
2 tablespoons olive oil
1/2 teaspoon garlic powder
1 teaspoon ground turmeric

Directions

Start by preheating your Air Fryer to 330 degrees F.
Toss the beets with the remaining ingredients and place them in the Air Fryer cooking basket.
Air fry your chips for 30 minutes, shaking the basket occasionally and working in batches.
Enjoy!

Cheese and Herb Stuffed Mushrooms

(Ready in about 10 minutes | Servings 4)

Per serving: 150 Calories; 10.7g Fat; 7.9g Carbs; 7.5g Protein; 2.5g Sugars; 1.3g Fiber

Ingredients

2 tablespoons olive oil
1/2 cup breadcrumbs
1/2 cup Parmesan cheese, grated
1 teaspoon garlic, minced
1 tablespoon fresh parsley, chopped
1 tablespoon fresh chives, chopped
Sea salt and freshly ground black pepper, to taste
1 pound button mushrooms, stems removed

Directions

In a mixing bowl, thoroughly combine the olive oil, breadcrumbs, Parmesan cheese, garlic, parsley, chives, salt, and black pepper.

Divide the filling between your mushrooms. Arrange the mushrooms in the Air Fryer basket.

Cook your mushrooms at 400 degrees F for about 7 minutes, shaking the basket halfway through the cooking time.

Bon appétit!

Classic Kale Chips

(Ready in about 10 minutes | Servings 4)

Per serving: 45 Calories; 3.5g Fat; 3g Carbs; 1.1g Protein; 0.9g Sugars; 0.8g Fiber

Ingredients

4 cups kale, torn into pieces
1 tablespoon sesame oil
1 teaspoon garlic powder
Sea salt and ground black pepper, to taste

Directions

Start by preheating your Air Fryer to 360 degrees F.

Toss the kale leaves with the remaining ingredients and place them in the Air Fryer cooking basket.

Air fry your chips for 8 minutes, shaking the basket occasionally and working in batches.

Enjoy!

Mini Bacon-Wrapped Sausages

(Ready in about 20 minutes | Servings 4)

Per serving: 540 Calories; 46.5g Fat; 8.9g Carbs; 21g Protein; 6.6g Sugars; 0.6g Fiber

Ingredients

1 pound mini sausages
2 tablespoons tamari sauce
2 tablespoons maple syrup
1 teaspoon chili powder
Ground black pepper, to taste
4 ounces bacon, thinly slices

Directions

Toss the mini sausages with the tamari sauce, maple syrup, chili powder, and black pepper.

Wrap the mini sausages with the bacon.

Place the sausages in a lightly oiled Air Fryer cooking basket.

Cook the sausages at 380 degrees F for 15 minutes, tossing the basket halfway through the cooking time.

Serve warm and enjoy!

Pigs in a Blanket

(Ready in about 10 minutes | Servings 6)

Per serving: 164 Calories; 6.2g Fat; 24.1g Carbs; 3.1g Protein; 3.2g Sugars; 1.5g Fiber

Ingredients

6 ounces crescent rolls, refrigerated
1 tablespoon mustard
10 ounces mini hot dogs

Directions

Separate the dough into triangles. Cut them lengthwise into 3 small triangles. Spread each triangle with mustard.

Place a mini hot dog on the shortest side of each triangle and roll it up.

Place the rolls in the Air Fryer cooking basket.

Bake the rolls at 320 degrees F for about 8 minutes, turning them over halfway through the cooking time.

Bon appétit!

Cheddar Cheese Cauliflower Bites

(Ready in about 15 minutes | Servings 4)

Per serving: 208 Calories; 12.2g Fat; 17.1g Carbs; 7.9g Protein; 3.9g Sugars; 3.1g Fiber

Ingredients

1 pound cauliflower, grated
1/2 cup cheddar cheese, shredded
1 ounce butter, room temperature
Sea salt and ground black pepper, to taste
1/2 cup tortilla chips, crushed
2 eggs whisked

Directions

Thoroughly combine all the ingredients in a mixing bowl. Shape the mixture into bite-sized balls.

Cook the cauliflower balls at 350 degrees F for about 13 minutes, turning them over halfway through the cooking time.

Bon appétit!

Sticky Pancetta-Wrapped Shrimp

(Ready in about 10 minutes | Servings 4)

Per serving: 118 Calories; 7.9g Fat; 7.1g Carbs; 4.5g Protein; 6.2g Sugars; 0.2g Fiber

Ingredients

12 shrimp, peeled and deveined
3 slicespancetta, cut into strips
2 tablespoons maple syrup
1 tablespoon Dijon mustard

Directions

Wrap the shrimp in the pancetta strips and toss them with the maple syrup and mustard.

Place the shrimp in a lightly greased Air Fryer cooking basket.

Cook the shrimp at 400 degrees F for 6 minutes, tossing the basket halfway through the cooking time.

Bon appétit!

Apple Pie Mini Rolls

(Ready in about 15 minutes | Servings 4)

Per serving: 344 Calories; 21.2g Fat; 33.4g Carbs; 6.3g Protein; 17g Sugars; 2.2g Fiber

Ingredients

6 ounces refrigerated crescent rolls

1 apple, peeled, cored, and grated

6 ounces cream cheese, crumbled

1/4 cup brown sugar

1 teaspoon apple pie spice

Directions

Separate the dough into rectangles. Mix the remaining ingredients until well combined.

Spread each rectangle with the cheese mixture; roll them up tightly. Place the rolls in the Air Fryer cooking basket.

Bake the rolls at 320 degrees F for about 5 minutes; turn them over and bake for a further 5 minutes.

Bon appétit!

Spicy Kale Crisps

(Ready in about 10 minutes | Servings 4)

Per serving: 48 Calories; 3.6g Fat; 3.6g Carbs; 1.2g Protein; 1g Sugars; 1.2g Fiber

Ingredients

5 cups kale leaves, torn into pieces, stems removed

1 tablespoon olive oil

1 teaspoon chili powder

Sea salt and ground black pepper, to taste

2 garlic cloves, minced

Directions

Start by preheating your Air Fryer to 360 degrees F.

Toss the kale leaves with the remaining ingredients and place them in the Air Fryer cooking basket.

Air fry the kale crisps for 8 minutes, shaking the basket occasionally and working in batches.

Enjoy!

Mediterranean-Style Beet Chips

(Ready in about 35 minutes | Servings 4)

Per serving: 89 Calories; 3.6g Fat; 12.4g Carbs; 2.2g Protein; 8g Sugars; 3.3g Fiber

Ingredients

1 pound red and yellow beets, peeled and sliced
1 tablespoon olive oil
Coarse sea salt and ground black pepper, to taste
1 teaspoon dried rosemary
1 teaspoon dried parsley flakes
1 teaspoon garlic
2 tablespoons scallions, chopped

Directions

Start by preheating your Air Fryer to 330 degrees F.
Toss the beets with the remaining ingredients and place them in the Air Fryer cooking basket.
Air fry your chips for 30 minutes, shaking the basket occasionally and working in batches.
Enjoy!

Southern-Fried Sweet Onion Rings

(Ready in about 10 minutes | Servings 4)

Per serving: 366 Calories; 9.3g Fat; 59g Carbs; 9.7g Protein; 9.3g Sugars; 4.1g Fiber

Ingredients

1/2 cup beer
1 cup plain flour
1 teaspoon baking powder
1 teaspoon cayenne pepper
Sea salt and ground black pepper, to taste
2 eggs, whisked
1 cup tortilla chips, crushed
2 sweet onions

Directions

Start by preheating your Air Fryer to 380 degrees F.
In a shallow bowl, mix the beer, flour, baking powder, cayenne pepper, salt, and black pepper.
Whisk the egg in another shallow bowl. Place the crushed tortilla chips in a separate bowl.
Dip the onion rings in the flour mixture, then in the eggs, then in the tortilla chips. Place the onion rings in the Air Fryer basket.
Cook the onion rings for about 8 minutes or until golden brown and cooked through.
Bon appétit!

Mexican-Style Tortilla Chips

(Ready in about 10 minutes | Servings 4)

Per serving: 88 Calories; 4.2g Fat; 11.7g Carbs; 1.5g Protein; 0.4g Sugars; 1.8g Fiber

Ingredients

4 corn tortillas, cut into wedges
1 tablespoon olive oil
1 tablespoon Mexican oregano
2 tablespoons lime juice
1 teaspoon chili powder
1 teaspoon ground cumin
Sea salt, to taste

Directions

Toss the tortilla wedges with the remaining ingredients.
Cook your tortilla chips at 360 degrees F for about 5 minutes or until crispy, working in batches.
Enjoy!

Gruyere Cheese-Stuffed Poblanos

(Ready in about 10 minutes | Servings 4)

Per serving: 242 Calories; 17.4g Fat; 10.4g Carbs; 13.2g Protein; 4.6g Sugars; 2.1g Fiber

Ingredients

8 poblano peppers, seeded and halved
4 ounces Gruyere cheese
4 ounces bacon, chopped

Directions

Stuff the peppers with the cheese and bacon; transfer them to a lightly oiled Air Fryer basket.
Air fry the peppers at 370 degrees for about 7 minutes or until golden brown.
Bon appétit!

Paprika Carrot Bites

(Ready in about 20 minutes | Servings 4)

Per serving: 113 Calories; 7.2g Fat; 12.4g Carbs; 1.2g Protein; 6g Sugars; 3.6g Fiber

Ingredients

1 pound carrots, cut into slices
2 tablespoons coconut oil
1 teaspoon paprika
1/2 teaspoon garlic powder
1/2 teaspoon dried oregano
1/2 teaspoon dried parsley flakes
Sea salt and ground black pepper, to taste

Directions

Toss the carrots with the remaining ingredients; then, arrange the carrots in the Air Fryer cooking basket.

Cook the carrots at 380 degrees F for 15 minutes, shaking the basket halfway through the cooking time.

Bon appétit!

Greek-Style Potato Wedges

(Ready in about 40 minutes | Servings 4)

Per serving: 153 Calories; 7g Fat; 21.2g Carbs; 2.6g Protein; 1.5g Sugars; 2.6g Fiber

Ingredients

1 pound potatoes, cut into wedges
2 tablespoons olive oil
Sea salt and ground black pepper, to taste
1 teaspoon paprika
1 teaspoon dried parsley flakes
1 teaspoon Greek seasoning mix

Directions

Start by preheating your Air Fryer to 400 degrees F.

Toss the potatoes with the remaining ingredients and place them in the Air Fryer cooking basket.

Air fry the potato wedges for 35 minutes, shaking the basket halfway through the cooking time.

Enjoy!

Asian Spare Ribs

(Ready in about 40 minutes | Servings 4)

Per serving: 153 Calories; 7g Fat; 21.2g Carbs; 2.6g Protein; 1.5g Sugars; 2.6g Fiber

Ingredients

2 pounds spare ribs
1/4 cup soy sauce
1/4 cup rice vinegar
1/4 cup sesame oil
2 garlic cloves, minced

Directions

Toss all ingredients in a lightly greased Air Fryer cooking basket.

Cook the ribs at 350 degrees F for 35 minutes, turning them over halfway through the cooking time.

Bon appétit!

Korean-Style Drumettes

(Ready in about 20 minutes | Servings 4)

Per serving: 304 Calories; 12.8g Fat; 22.4g Carbs; 24.5g Protein; 20.5g Sugars; 0.7g Fiber

Ingredients

1 pound chicken drumettes
4 tablespoons soy sauce
1/4 cup rice vinegar
4 tablespoons honey
2 tablespoons sesame oil
1 teaspoon Gochugaru, Korean chili powder
2 tablespoons scallions, chopped
2 garlic cloves, minced

Directions

Toss the chicken drumettes with the remaining ingredients.

Cook the chicken drumettes at 380 degrees F for 18 minutes, turning them over halfway through the cooking time.

Bon appétit!

Mozzarella Eggplant Chips

(Ready in about 20 minutes | Servings 4)

Per serving: 129 Calories; 6g Fat; 9.3g Carbs; 10.4g Protein; 5.1g Sugars; 4.3g Fiber

Ingredients

1 pound eggplant, cut into slices
2 tablespoons butter, melted
1/2 teaspoon smoked paprika
1 teaspoon Italian seasoning
Sea salt and ground black pepper, to taste
1 cup mozzarella cheese, shredded

Directions

Toss the eggplant with the butter and spices. Arrange the eggplant slices in the Air Fryer basket.

Cook the eggplant at 400 degrees F for about 15 minutes, shaking the basket halfway through the cooking time.

Bon appétit!

Hot Zucchini Fries

(Ready in about 15 minutes | Servings 4)

Per serving: 227 Calories; 17.6g Fat; 9.3g Carbs; 10.8g Protein; 1.2g Sugars; 3.1g Fiber

Ingredients

1 pound zucchini, cut into sticks
1/2 cup Parmesan cheese
1/2 cup almond flour
1 egg, whisked
2 tablespoons olive oil
1 teaspoon hot paprika
Sea salt and ground black pepper, to taste

Directions

Start by preheating your Air Fryer to 390 degrees F.

Toss the zucchini sticks with the remaining ingredients and arrange them in a single layer in the Air Fryer cooking basket.

Cook the zucchini sticks for about 10 minutes at 390 degrees F, shaking the basket halfway through the cooking time. Work in batches.

Bon appétit!

Red Beet Chips

(Ready in about 35 minutes | Servings 4)

Per serving: 79 Calories; 3.6g Fat; 10.4g Carbs; 1.8g Protein; 7.2g Sugars; 3.2g Fiber

Ingredients

1 pound red beets, peeled and cut into 1/8-inch slices

1 tablespoon olive oil

1 teaspoon cayenne pepper

Sea salt and ground black pepper, to taste

Directions

Start by preheating your Air Fryer to 330 degrees F.

Toss the beets with the remaining ingredients and place them in the Air Fryer cooking basket.

Air fry your chips for 30 minutes, shaking the basket occasionally and working in batches.

Enjoy!

Ginger and Honey Wings

(Ready in about 20 minutes | Servings 4)

Per serving: 404 Calories; 13.4g Fat; 18.3g Carbs; 50.1g Protein; 18.3g Sugars; 0.3g Fiber

Ingredients

2 pounds chicken wings

1/4 cup honey

2 tablespoons fish sauce

2 garlic cloves, crushed

1 teaspoon ginger, peeled and grated

2 tablespoons butter, melted

Sea salt and ground black pepper, to taste

Directions

Toss the chicken wings with the remaining ingredients.

Cook the chicken wings at 380 degrees F for 18 minutes, turning them over halfway through the cooking time.

Bon appétit!

VEGAN

Fried Green Beans

(Ready in about 10 minutes | Servings 3)

Per serving: 174 Calories; 13.1g Fat; 12.2g Carbs; 4.9g Protein; 4.8g Sugars; 4g Fiber

Ingredients

3/4 pound green beans, trimmed and halved
1/2 cup vegan mayonnaise
1 teaspoon granulated garlic
1 teaspoon paprika
Kosher salt and ground black pepper, to taste

Directions

Toss the green beans with the remaining ingredients until well coated on all sides.
Air fry the green beans at 390 degrees F for about 6 minutes, tossing the basket halfway through the cooking time.
Enjoy!

Greek-Style Vegan Burgers

(Ready in about 20 minutes | Servings 4)

Per serving: 169 Calories; 4.1g Fat; 26.8g Carbs; 8.2g Protein; 4.9g Sugars; 8.2g Fiber

Ingredients

1 tablespoon ground chia seeds
14 ounces canned chickpeas, rinsed and drained
1/4 cup fresh coriander
1/4 cup fresh scallions
1 tablespoon rosemary
1 tablespoon thyme
1 tablespoon basil
2 garlic cloves, peeled
1/2 teaspoon ground cumin
Sea salt and ground black pepper, to taste
2 tablespoons fresh lemon juice

Directions

To make a flax egg, soak the ground flaxseeds in 2 tablespoons of water for 15 minutes.
In your blender or food processor, mix all the ingredients, including the flax egg, until everything is well incorporated.
Form the mixture into patties and place them in a lightly greased Air Fryer cooking basket.
Air fry the patties at 380 degrees F for about 15 minutes, turning them over halfway through the cooking time.
Bon appétit!

Golden Parsnip Sticks

(Ready in about 20 minutes | Servings 4)

Per serving: 169 Calories; 4.1g Fat; 26.8g Carbs; 8.2g Protein; 4.9g Sugars; 8.2g Fiber

Ingredients

1 pound parsnip, trimmed and cut into sticks
2 tablespoons olive oil
1 teaspoon garlic, minced
1 teaspoon turmeric powder
1 tablespoon Dijon mustard
Sea salt and ground black pepper, to taste

Directions

Toss the parsnip with the remaining ingredients; place them in the Air Fryer cooking basket.

Cook the parsnip sticks at 400 degrees F for about 15 minutes, shaking the basket occasionally to ensure even cooking.

Serve warm and enjoy!

Broccoli Vegan Tempura

(Ready in about 10 minutes | Servings 4)

Per serving: 232 Calories; 7.6g Fat; 33.8g Carbs; 6.9g Protein; 2.6g Sugars; 4.3g Fiber

Ingredients

1 cup all-purpose flour
1/2 cup beer
2 tablespoons sesame oil
1/2 teaspoon cayenne pepper
1 teaspoon chili powder
Sea salt and ground black pepper, to taste
1 pound broccoli florets

Directions

In a mixing bowl, thoroughly combine the flour, beer, oil, and spices.

Dip the broccoli florets in the tempura mixture and place them in a lightly oiled Air Fryer cooking basket.

Cook the broccoli florets at 395 degrees F for 6 minutes, shaking the basket halfway through the cooking time.

Bon appétit!

Classic Chickpea Burgers

(Ready in about 20 minutes | Servings 4)

Per serving: 281 Calories; 9.8g Fat; 38.2g Carbs; 11.1g Protein; 7.2g Sugars; 9g Fiber

Ingredients

16 ounces chickpeas, boiled and drained
2 tablespoons all-purpose flour
1/2 teaspoon baking soda
1/4 cup fresh parsley leaves, stems removed
1/4 cup fresh cilantro leaves, stems removed
1 teaspoon green chili paste
1 onion, quartered
4 garlic cloves, peeled
Sea salt and ground black pepper, to taste
2 tablespoons olive oil

Directions

Pulse all the ingredients in your food processor until everything is well incorporated.

Form the mixture into burgers and place them in a lightly greased Air Fryer cooking basket.

Cook the burgers at 380 degrees F for about 15 minutes, turning them occasionally to ensure even cooking.

Serve with burger buns and enjoy!

DESSERTS

Homemade Chocolate Eclairs

(Ready in about 30 minutes | Servings 4)

Per serving: 403 Calories; 29.6g Fat; 28.6g Carbs; 7.7g Protein; 9.1g Sugars; 1.4g Fiber

Ingredients

Choux Pastry:

3/4 cup all-purpose flour

1/4 cup almond milk

1/2 cup water

6 tablespoons butter, room temperature

1 teaspoon brown sugar

1/4 teaspoon kosher salt

1/4 teaspoon grated nutmeg

3 eggs

Chocolate Glaze:

1/3 cup heavy whipping cream

2 ounces semi-sweet chocolate chips

Directions

In a mixing bowl, thoroughly combine all the ingredients for the pastry. Place the batter in a piping bag fitted with a large open star tip.

Pipe your eclairs into strips and lower them onto the greased Air Fryer pan.

Cook your eclairs in the preheated Air Fryer at 360 degrees F for 10 minutes, flipping them halfway through the cooking time.

Repeat with the remaining batter. Place the eclairs in your refrigerator while making the chocolate glaze.

Heat the whipping cream in a microwave; add in the chocolate and whisk until smooth sauce forms.

Top the chilled eclairs with the chocolate glaze and let it sit for about 30 minutes before serving. Bon appétit!

Autumn Pear Pancake

(Ready in about 15 minutes | Servings 4)

Per serving: 183 Calories; 6.6g Fat; 24.6g Carbs; 5.7g Protein; 10.1g Sugars; 2.1g Fiber

Ingredients

1 pear, peeled, cored and sliced
1 tablespoon lemon juice
1 tablespoon coconut oil
1/2 cup all-purpose flour
1/2 teaspoon baking powder
2 tablespoons brown sugar
1/2 teaspoon cinnamon
2 eggs, whisked
1/2 cup milk
1/2 teaspoon vanilla extract

Directions

Drizzle the pear slices with the lemon juice and melted coconut oil; arrange the pear slices in a baking pan.

Mix the remaining ingredients to make the batter. Pour the batter over the pears. Transfer the baking pan to the Air Fryer cooking basket.

Bake your pancake at 350 degrees F for about 13 minutes or until it is golden brown around the edges.

Bon appétit!

Colorful Fruit Kabobs

(Ready in about 15 minutes | Servings 4)

Per serving: 167 Calories; 7g Fat; 27.6g Carbs; 1.3g Protein; 22.1g Sugars; 2.3g Fiber

Ingredients

1 cup melon, cut into 1-inch chunks
1 cup pineapple, cut into 1-inch chunks
1 banana, cut into 1-inch chunks
1 peach, cut into 1-inch chunks
2 tablespoons coconut oil, melted
2 tablespoons honey

Directions

Toss your fruits with the coconut oil and honey.

Thread the fruits onto skewers and place them in the Air Fryer cooking basket.

Then, cook the skewers at 400 degrees F for approximately 10 minutes, turning them over halfway through the cooking time.

Bon appétit!

Favorite Almond Cupcakes

(Ready in about 20 minutes | Servings 6)

Per serving: 373 Calories; 24.6g Fat; 33.6g Carbs; 7.7g Protein; 18.1g Sugars; 2.7g Fiber

Ingredients

3/4 cup self-raising flour

1/4 cup cocoa powder

2 eggs, beaten

1 stick butter, at room temperature

1 cup granulated sugar

1/2 cup almond milk

2 ounces almonds, slivered

Directions

Start by preheating your Air Fryer to 330 degrees F.

Mix all the ingredients in a bowl. Scrape the batter into silicone baking molds; place them in the Air Fryer basket.

Bake your cupcakes for about 15 minutes or until a tester comes out dry and clean.

Allow the cupcakes to cool before unmolding and serving. Bon appétit!

Mini Monkey Rolls

(Ready in about 25 minutes | Servings 4)

Per serving: 383 Calories; 16.6g Fat; 52g Carbs; 7.4g Protein; 13.6g Sugars; 3.7g Fiber

Ingredients

12 ounces refrigerated dinner roll dough

1/2 cup brown sugar

1 teaspoon ground cinnamon

1/4 cup almonds, chopped

1/4 cup butter, melted

Directions

Spritz muffin cups with a nonstick cooking spray.

Separate the dough into biscuits. In a shallow bowl, thoroughly combine the sugar, cinnamon, almonds, and butter.

Roll the biscuits over the sugar/cinnamon mixture. Divide them between muffin cups.

Bake the mini monkey rolls at 340 degrees F for about 20 minutes or until golden brown. Turn them upside down and serve.

Indian Vettu Cake

(Ready in about 15 minutes | Servings 4)

Per serving: 225 Calories; 9g Fat; 30.7g Carbs; 5.2g Protein; 12.3g Sugars; 0.8g Fiber

Ingredients

3/4 cup all-purpose flour
1/2 teaspoon baking powder
1/4 teaspoon cardamom powder
1/4 teaspoon cinnamon powder
2 eggs, whisked
1/2 cup caster sugar
2 tablespoons coconut oil

Directions

Mix all the ingredients to make the batter. Pour the batter into a lightly oiled baking pan.
Place the pan in the Air Fryer cooking basket.
Air fry your fritters at 350 degrees F for about 13 minutes or until they are golden brown around the edges.
Bon appétit!

Harvest Apple Cake

(Ready in about 20 minutes | Servings 3)

Per serving: 215 Calories; 5.7g Fat; 34.7g Carbs; 6.2g Protein; 19.8g Sugars; 3.6g Fiber

Ingredients

1/3 cup all-purpose flour
1/4 cup coconut flour
1/2 teaspoon baking powder
1/2 teaspoon ground cinnamon
3 tablespoons brown sugar
A pinch of kosher salt
2 eggs, beaten
1/2 teaspoon pure vanilla extract
1/4 cup full-fat milk
2 small apples, peeled, cored, and grated

Directions

Mix all the ingredients to make the batter. Pour the batter into a lightly oiled baking pan.
Place the pan in the Air Fryer cooking basket.
Bake your cake at 350 degrees F for about 13 minutes or until it is golden brown around the edges.
Bon appétit!

Mini Maraschino Cherry Pies

(Ready in about 25 minutes | Servings 6)

Per serving: 265 Calories; 9.7g Fat; 41.7g Carbs; 3.3g Protein; 22.2g Sugars; 1.6g Fiber

Ingredients

1/2 cup Maraschino cherries, pitted
1/2 cup granulated sugar
1/2 teaspoon ground cardamom
1 teaspoon pure vanilla extract
2 tablespoons hazelnuts, chopped
12 ounces refrigerated flaky cinnamon rolls

Directions

Toss the cherries with the sugar, cardamom, vanilla, and hazelnuts.

Spray muffin cups with a nonstick cooking spray. Separate the dough into 6 rolls and press them into the prepared muffin cups.

Spoon the filling into each dough-lined cup.

Bake the mini pies at 350 degrees F for 20 minutes or until the top is golden brown. Bon appétit!

Fluffy Blueberry Fritters

(Ready in about 15 minutes | Servings 4)

Per serving: 195 Calories; 8g Fat; 25.4g Carbs; 4.9g Protein; 6.9g Sugars; 1g Fiber

Ingredients

3/4 cup all-purpose flour
1 teaspoon baking powder
1/2 cup coconut milk
2 tablespoons coconut sugar
A pinch of sea salt
1 egg
2 tablespoons melted butter
2 ounces fresh blueberries

Directions

In a mixing bowl, thoroughly combine all the ingredients.

Drop a spoonful of batter onto the greased Air Fryer pan. Cook in the preheated Air Fryer at 360 degrees F for 10 minutes, flipping them halfway through the cooking time.

Repeat with the remaining batter and serve warm. Enjoy!

Cranberry Chocolate Cupcakes

(Ready in about 20 minutes | Servings 6)

Per serving: 545 Calories; 35.1g Fat; 54.4g Carbs; 6.2g Protein; 36g Sugars; 3.1g Fiber

Ingredients

Cupcakes:
3/4 cup self-raising flour
3/4 cup caster sugar
1/4 cup cocoa powder
A pinch of sea salt
A pinch of grated nutmeg
2 eggs, whisked
1/2 cup buttermilk
1/2 stick butter, melted
2 ounces dried cranberries
Frosting:
1/2 cup butter, room temperature
1 teaspoon vanilla extract
3 ounces chocolate chips, melted
4 tablespoons heavy whipping cream

Directions

Start by preheating your Air Fryer to 330 degrees F.
Mix all the ingredients for the cupcakes. Scrape the batter into silicone baking molds; place them in the Air Fryer basket.
Bake your cupcakes for about 15 minutes or until a tester comes out dry and clean.
Beat all the ingredients for the frosting using an electric mixer. Pipe the frosting onto the cupcakes. Bon appétit!

Indian-Style Unnakai Malabar

(Ready in about 15 minutes | Servings 1)

Per serving: 545 Calories; 35.1g Fat; 54.4g Carbs; 6.2g Protein; 36g Sugars; 3.1g Fiber

Ingredients

1 plantain, peeled

1/4 cup coconut flakes

1/4 teaspoon cinnamon powder

1/4 teaspoon cardamom powder

1 tablespoon ghee

2 tablespoons brown sugar

Directions

Preheat your Air Fryer to 390 degrees F.

Toss the plantain with the remaining ingredients.

Bake the prepared plantain in the preheated Air Fryer approximately 13 minutes, flipping it halfway through the cooking time.

Bon appétit!

Squash Fried Cake

(Ready in about 15 minutes | Servings 4)

Per serving: 155 Calories; 5.7g Fat; 20.4g Carbs; 5.2g Protein; 1.6g Sugars; 1.9g Fiber

Ingredients

2 cups butternut squash, shredded

1/2 cup all-purpose flour

2 eggs, beaten

1 tablespoon coconut oil

1 teaspoon pumpkin pie spice mix

Directions

In a mixing bowl, thoroughly combine all the ingredients.

Drop a spoonful of batter onto the greased Air Fryer pan. Cook in the preheated Air Fryer at 360 degrees F for 10 minutes, flipping them halfway through the cooking time.

Repeat with the remaining batter and serve warm. Enjoy!

Honey and Coconut Apricots

(Ready in about 20 minutes | Servings 4)

Per serving: 176 Calories; 6.8g Fat; 28.4g Carbs; 2.8g Protein; 26g Sugars; 1.8g Fiber

Ingredients

8 apricots, halved and pitted
1 tablespoon coconut oil, melted
2 tablespoons honey
1 teaspoon ground cinnamon
2 ounces mascarpone cheese
1 tablespoon coconut flakes

Directions

Toss the apricots with the coconut oil, honey, and cinnamon.

Place the apricots in a lightly oiled Air Fryer cooking basket.

Cook the apricots at 340 degrees F for 16 minutes. Top the fried apricots with mascarpone cheese and coconut flakes.

Bon appétit!

Danish Cinnamon Rolls

(Ready in about 15 minutes | Servings 4)

Per serving: 356 Calories; 20.3g Fat; 39.4g Carbs; 2.8g Protein; 24.2g Sugars; 1.1g Fiber

Ingredients

9 ounces refrigerated crescent rolls
1 tablespoon coconut oil
4 tablespoons caster sugar
1 teaspoon ground cinnamon

Directions

Separate the dough into rectangles. Mix the remaining ingredients until well combined.

Spread each rectangle with the cinnamon mixture; roll them up tightly.

Place the rolls in the Air Fryer cooking basket.

Bake the rolls at 300 degrees F for about 5 minutes; turn them over and bake for a further 5 minutes.

Bon appétit!

Festive Rum Fritters

(Ready in about 25 minutes | Servings 4)

Per serving: 235 Calories; 11.7g Fat; 26.7g Carbs; 3g Protein; 5.6g Sugars; 1.4g Fiber

Ingredients

3/4 cup all-purpose flour

3/4 cup water

1 tablespoon rum

4 tablespoons butter

1 banana, mashed

1 tablespoon caster sugar

1/4 teaspoon salt

1/4 teaspoon grated nutmeg

Directions

In a mixing bowl, thoroughly combine all the ingredients.

Drop a spoonful of batter onto the greased Air Fryer pan. Cook in the preheated Air Fryer at 360 degrees F for 10 minutes, flipping them halfway through the cooking time.

Repeat with the remaining batter and serve warm. Enjoy!

Vanilla Mug Cake

(Ready in about 25 minutes | Servings 1)

Per serving: 476 Calories; 39g Fat; 28.5g Carbs; 8.8g Protein; 7g Sugars; 6.2g Fiber

Ingredients

2 tablespoons all-purpose flour

2 tablespoons almond flour

2 tablespoons cocoa powder, unsweetened

2 tablespoons agave nectar

1/4 teaspoon baking powder

1 teaspoon pure vanilla extract

A pinch of kosher salt

A pinch of grated nutmeg

2 tablespoons coconut oil, at room temperature

2 tablespoons full-fat milk

Directions

Start by preheating your Air Fryer to 350 degrees F.

Thoroughly combine all the ingredients; mix until well combined.

Spoon the mixture into a mug and place it in the Air Fryer cooking basket.

Air fry the mug cake for approximately 20 minutes. Bon appétit!

Grandma's Fried Banana

(Ready in about 20 minutes | Servings 1)

Per serving: 286 Calories; 14.9g Fat; 43.5g Carbs; 1.3g Protein; 30.7g Sugars; 3.8g Fiber

Ingredients

1 banana, peeled and sliced
1 tablespoon coconut oil
2 tablespoons granulated sugar
1/2 teaspoon ground cloves
1/2 teaspoon ground cinnamon

Directions

Preheat your Air Fryer to 390 degrees F.
Toss banana slices with the remaining ingredients.
Bake the prepared banana slices in the preheated Air Fryer approximately 13 minutes, flipping them halfway through the cooking time.
Bon appétit!

OTHER AIR FRYER FAVORITES

Spinach Quiche with Canadian Bacon

(Ready in about 20 minutes | Servings 4)

Per serving: 220 Calories; 11.3g Fat; 12.5g Carbs; 16.4g Protein; 2.6g Sugars; 1.6g Fiber

Ingredients

6 eggs, whisked
6 tablespoons all-purpose flour
1/2 teaspoon baking soda
6 tablespoons full-fat milk
4 ounces Canadian bacon, diced
1 tablespoon olive oil
2 cups baby spinach
1 tomato, chopped
1 Serrano peppers, chopped
Kosher salt and freshly ground black pepper, to taste

Directions

Start by preheating your Air Fryer to 350 degrees F. Then, spritz the sides and bottom of a baking pan with a nonstick cooking oil.
In a mixing bowl, thoroughly combine all the ingredients.
Pour the mixture into the prepared baking pan and lower the pan into the Air Fryer basket.
Cook your frittata in the preheated Air Fryer for approximately 15 minutes, or until a toothpick comes out dry and clean.
Bon appétit!

Indian-Style Dosas

(Ready in about 20 minutes | Servings 4)

Per serving: 176 Calories; 6.1g Fat; 24.1g Carbs; 5.3g Protein; 6.3g Sugars; 0.6g Fiber

Ingredients

1/2 cup all-purpose flour
1/2 cup rice flour
1/2 teaspoon baking powder
1/2 cup water
1 clove garlic, minced
1/2 teaspoon ground turmeric
1/2 teaspoon ground cumin
1/2 teaspoon mustard seeds

Directions

Thoroughly combine all the ingredients in a mixing bowl.
Drop a spoonful of batter onto the greased Air Fryer pan.
Cook the cakes in the preheated Air Fryer at 360 degrees F for 10 minutes, flipping them halfway through the cooking time.
Repeat with the remaining batter and serve warm.
Bon appétit!

German Königsberger Klopse

(Ready in about 20 minutes | Servings 4)

Per serving: 256 Calories; 14.6g Fat; 8.7g Carbs; 22.3g Protein; 1g Sugars; 0.8g Fiber

Ingredients

1/3 pound ground beef
1/2 pound ground turkey
1 egg, slightly beaten
1/4 cup tortilla chips, crushed
1/2 cup cheddar cheese, grated
1 small onion, chopped
1 teaspoon garlic, minced
Sea salt and fresh ground black pepper, to taste
1 teaspoon dried parsley flakes
1 teaspoon dried oregano
1 teaspoon dried basil

Directions

Mix all the ingredients until everything is well combined. Form the mixture into balls.
Cook the meatballs at 380 degrees F for about 15 minutes or until cooked through, shaking the basket halfway through the cooking time.
Bon appétit!

Easy Cinnamon Toast

(Ready in about 10 minutes | Servings 2)

Per serving: 168 Calories; 12.2g Fat; 11g Carbs; 1.9g Protein; 1.7g Sugars; 1.2g Fiber

Ingredients

2 bread slices

1 teaspoon ground cinnamon

2 tablespoons butter, softened

Directions

Toss the bread slices with cinnamon and butter.

Air Fryer the bread slices at 330 degrees F for about 4 minutes; turn them over and cook for a further 3 to 4 minutes.

Bon appétit!

Easy Birthday Tartlets

(Ready in about 20 minutes | Servings 4)

Per serving: 220 Calories; 17g Fat; 4.4g Carbs; 12.6g Protein; 2.5g Sugars; 0.7g Fiber

Ingredients

5 eggs

2 tablespoons butter, room temperature

1 cup baby spinach

1 bell pepper, chopped

1 shallot, chopped

Kosher salt ground black pepper, to taste

1/2 teaspoon dried basil

1/2 teaspoon dried oregano

3 ounces feta cheese, crumbled

Directions

Start by preheating your Air Fryer to 350 degrees F. Then, spritz mini muffin cups with a nonstick cooking oil.

In a mixing bowl, thoroughly combine all the ingredients.

Pour the mixture into the prepared mini muffin cups and lower them into the Air Fryer basket.

Cook your tartlets in the preheated Air Fryer for approximately 15 minutes, or until a toothpick comes out dry and clean.

Bon appétit!

Breakfast Waffle with Blueberries

(Ready in about 10 minutes | Servings 1)

Per serving: 134 Calories; 7g Fat; 16.4g Carbs; 2.7g Protein; 3.1g Sugars; 1g Fiber

Ingredients

1 frozen waffle

1 tablespoon blueberries

1 tablespoon whipped cream

Directions

Place the frozen waffle in a lightly greased Air Fryer cooking basket.

Air fry your waffle at 360 degrees F for 7 minutes, turning it over halfway through the cooking time.

Serve your waffle with blueberries and whipped cream. Bon appétit!

Roasted Green Bean Salad

(Ready in about 10 minutes | Servings 4)

Per serving: 204 Calories; 16.7g Fat; 10.4g Carbs; 4.5g Protein; 5.1g Sugars; 3.4g Fiber

Ingredients

1 pound green beans, trimmed

Sea salt and ground black pepper, to taste

1 shallot, finely chopped

1 teaspoon garlic, minced

1/4 cup extra-virgin olive oil

2 tablespoons white wine vinegar

1/4 cup fresh parsley, chopped

2 ounces feta cheese, crumbled

Directions

Arrange the green beans in a lightly greased Air Fryer basket.

Cook the green beans at 375 degrees F for 7 minutes; make sure to check the green beans halfway through the cooking time.

Add the green beans to a salad bowl; add in the remaining ingredients and stir to combine well. Enjoy!

Classic Corn Salad

(Ready in about 15 minutes | Servings 2)

Per serving: 259 Calories; 19g Fat; 23.4g Carbs; 3.9g Protein; 5.6g Sugars; 3.4g Fiber

Ingredients

2 corn on the cob, husked and halved

2 teaspoons ghee

Sea salt and ground black pepper, to taste

1 Vidalia onion, thinly sliced

1 bell pepper, thinly sliced

2 tablespoons lime juice

2 tablespoons extra-virgin olive oil

Directions

Toss the ears of corn with the ghee, salt, and pepper. Arrange the ears of corn in the Air Fryer cooking basket.

Cook the ears of corn at 390 degrees F for about 10 minutes, tossing them halfway through the cooking time.

Next, cut the kernels off the cob. Toss the corn kernels with the remaining ingredients. Bon appétit!

Roasted Ranch Garbanzo Beans

(Ready in about 15 minutes | Servings 4)

Per serving: 159 Calories; 5.9g Fat; 20.4g Carbs; 6g Protein; 3.6g Sugars; 5.7g Fiber

Ingredients

12 ounces canned garbanzo beans, drained and rinsed

1 tablespoon olive oil

1 tablespoon Ranch seasoning mix

Directions

Toss the garbanzo beans with the other ingredients in the Air Fryer cooking basket.

Air fry your garbanzo beans at 390 degrees F for about 13 minutes, tossing the basket a couple of times.

Bon appétit!

Authentic Italian Arancini

(Ready in about 20 minutes | Servings 4)

Per serving: 248 Calories; 12.5g Fat; 23.7g Carbs; 9.4g Protein; 0.8g Sugars; 2g Fiber

Ingredients

1 ½ cups cooked Arborio rice
1/2 cup Parmesan cheese, grated
1 cup panko crumbs
2 large eggs, whisked
1 teaspoon dried parsley flakes
Kosher salt and freshly ground black pepper, to taste
2 tablespoons butter

Directions

Start by preheating your Air Fryer to 380 degrees F.

Mix all the ingredients until everything is well combined. Form the mixture into balls.

Air fry the balls for about 15 minutes or until cooked through, shaking the basket halfway through the cooking time.

Bon appétit!

Classic Vegetarian Frittata

(Ready in about 20 minutes | Servings 4)

Per serving: 320 Calories; 24.3g Fat; 4.5g Carbs; 19.4g Protein; 1.8g Sugars; 0.6g Fiber

Ingredients

8 eggs
6 tablespoons sour cream
Coarse sea salt and ground black pepper, to taste
1 teaspoon cayenne pepper
1/2 teaspoon dried oregano
1 teaspoon dried basil
4 ounces gouda cheese, shredded
2 tablespoons olive oil
1 small zucchini, shredded
1 small shallot, chopped

Directions

Start by preheating your Air Fryer to 350 degrees F. Then, spritz the sides and bottom of a baking pan with a nonstick cooking oil.

In a mixing bowl, thoroughly combine all the ingredients.

Pour the mixture into the prepared baking pan and lower the pan into the Air Fryer basket.

Cook your frittata in the preheated Air Fryer for approximately 15 minutes, or until a toothpick comes out dry and clean.

Bon appétit!

Parmesan Potato Croquettes

(Ready in about 20 minutes | Servings 4)

Per serving: 273 Calories; 12.9g Fat; 30.2g Carbs; 10g Protein; 1.4g Sugars; 2.7g Fiber

Ingredients

1/2 cup flour
1 teaspoon baking powder
3/4 pounds potatoes, grated
2 eggs, whisked
1/2 cup parmesan cheese, grated
1 tablespoon parsley, chopped
1 tablespoon cilantro, chopped
1 tablespoon chives, chopped
1 teaspoon smoked paprika
Kosher salt and ground black pepper, to taste
2 tablespoons olive oil

Directions

Mix all the ingredients in a bowl. Shape the mixture into bite-sized balls and place them in a lightly oiled Air Fryer cooking basket.

Cook your croquettes at 400 degrees F for about 14 minutes, shaking the basket halfway through the cooking time.

Bon appétit!

Egg Salad Sandwich

(Ready in about 25 minutes | Servings 3)

Per serving: 503 Calories; 27.7g Fat; 40.2g Carbs; 23.4g Protein; 6.6g Sugars; 6.5g Fiber

Ingredients

6 eggs
2 tablespoons scallions, chopped
2 garlic cloves, minced
1/4 cup sour cream
1/4 cup mayonnaise
1 teaspoon yellow mustard
Sea salt and ground black pepper, to taste
1 garlic clove, minced
6 slices whole-grain bread

Directions

Place the eggs in the Air Fryer cooking basket.

Air fry your eggs at 270 degrees F for about 15 minutes.

Peel and chop the eggs; place them in a salad bowl and add in the remaining ingredients. Gently toss to combine.

Next, air fry the bread slices at 330 degrees F for about 4 minutes; turn them over and cook for a further 3 to 4 minutes.

Lastly, assemble your sandwiches with the egg salad and toasted bread.

Bon appétit!

APPENDIX : RECIPES INDEX